WHEN YOUR **MATE** HAS

emotionally

CHECKED OUT

radical steps to
transform
your relationship

Craig A. Miller

TATE PUBLISHING, LLC

TABLE OF CONTENTS

PREFACE

T here is a widespread and devastating problem in our homes today that is difficult to recognize and rarely understood. The problem occurs when one mate has difficulty showing and receiving emotions, love, and affection, leaving the other family members to exist in a world of loneliness, disappointment, and disrespect. If there is little opportunity to communicate thoughts and feelings in the marriage relationship, the unloved mate believes the only choices are to resign to living in an unsatisfying relationship or decide to become one more divorce statistic. Living with someone that is emotionally unavailable is a very common, yet subtle, form of disrespect. This disrespect is often misunderstood and is a destructive problem of major proportions that is hard for couples to identify, with little-known solutions—until now.

When Your Mate Has Emotionally Checked Out is for people living in relationships where the lack of emotions, love, and respect continues despite repeated unsuccessful efforts to change the relationship through praying, loving, waiting, complaining, and counseling. This book candidly addresses how the lack of emotion destroys the ability to have heartfelt love and gives radical solutions to bring the emotions, love, and respect back into the relationship. This book also provides valuable insights, individual examples, inspiring scriptures, and powerful techniques to learn why a person becomes emotionally unavailable or unemotional, and teaches you how to help them emotionally relate the way they were originally created. Most importantly, the unloved partner will be empowered to do these things: respond differently to the unemotional mate; overcome the frustration of living with the stubborn attitudes of a selfish mate; and change the unemotional mate's mind without the emotional mate losing his or her own heart, mind, and soul in the process.

It is also important to understand that the characteristics of people whom I call "emotionally unavailable or unemotional" are very similar in nature and will be discussed in detail in this book. These people have difficulty showing healthy emotions and are unable to provide healthy encouragement or support when others express emotions. However, one difference is that the emotionally unavailable individual would have the tendency to demonstrate various types of negative emotions, such as anger. In order to make it easier for the reader, the term "unemotional mate" will be used throughout the book to combine the problems and solutions for both the emotionally unavailable and unemotional individuals. The term "emotional mate" will be used to refer to the unloved partner who is struggling to change the unemotional mate. To help apply this information, case examples have been written from the stories I have heard over the years. The names used in each example are fictitious, but the examples are real to emphasize that you are not alone and there is hope with your struggles.

I would like to thank God as the source of my knowledge and direction for this book. I am also grateful for the many friends who have been prayerfully supportive and helpful in providing suggestions and encouragement throughout my writing. I want to especially thank my wife and two boys for their patience and love throughout my learning and writing. And finally, it is my hope and prayer that the reader will find the emotion, love, and respect that he or she deserves from what God originally intended in every relationship.

PART I

where have all the feelings gone?

I

STRUGGLING TO HAVE A RELATIONSHIP

*Someone to tell it to is one of the
fundamental needs of human beings.*
—Miles Franklin

As Mary was sitting at the kitchen table sipping a cup of coffee, her mind drifted to people she thought of calling. *Oh, forget it,* she thought to herself, *I wouldn't want to burden them.* To escape the familiar feelings of loneliness and sadness, she began thinking of all the things she had to do that day. She rationalized that her friends were busy people, her spouse worked hard, and it was important that she accomplish her own activities. *After all,* she reminded herself, *I've struggled with finding meaningful relationships for so long, why should I expect them now?*

Mary could not escape the gnawing emptiness she felt deep inside. Pushing away these feelings over the years was beginning to take its toll. She knew this wasn't what she wanted, but she didn't know how to change it. Deep inside there existed a strong yearning, like an ache in her chest, to share an emotional connection with someone in her life. She longed for conversation about things that mattered, with people who were important to her. Mary yearned for someone to share the burdens of her heart and the treasured moments of her day. She wondered if having those heartfelt conversations would ease the emptiness inside and help her to feel better about herself. Mary believed it was possible to have love and acceptance in close relationships, but couldn't understand why it was such a struggle to make it happen.

A grumbling noise from the other room brought Mary out of her deep thoughts. Mary looked up to see her husband, Phil, complaining to the guy on the television. Seeing Phil slouched in the chair brought a flood of thoughts and emotions. Mary wanted to scream out, *Why aren't you sitting in here looking at me instead of having a relationship with that idiot box? Why don't you talk to me about things that matter in life?* For years, she tried to overcome the anguish she felt over feeling ignored. To Mary, it seemed that her husband always had more to do or say to others than to her. *What is wrong with me?* she thought to herself. Mary couldn't remember the last time she had a meaningful dialogue with Phil about a subject that mattered. When Phil did not talk to her it was as if he were saying, "You're not important, and this relationship doesn't matter." The more she grieved about what was missing in their relationship, the deeper her hurt and disappointment grew. Looking at the clock, Mary realized she was running late for an appointment. Just like so many times before, Mary pushed the ugly feelings aside, so she could get on with the day.

WHEN DREAMS ARE CRUSHED

Loneliness has become an increasing problem in our relationships today. Relationships are becoming lonelier as people are turning inward instead of reaching out to others. Our ability to share what is in our hearts and on our minds is becoming a lost art. Like Mary, when you are living in a relationship without receiving love or being able to express heartfelt thoughts and feelings, you struggle to have a meaningful relationship. Mary's heartache and loneliness resulted from her disappointment at not having her dreams fulfilled by the most important person in her life. Mary wanted what everyone yearns for and what everyone desires in a relationship: to be loved, accepted, respected, and appreciated by another person. However, when you don't receive those desires your dreams can be crushed. It would be natural to dream of having these basic human desires met by your mate, but disappointing to have those dreams crushed because your mate is incapable of fulfilling them.

If you live long enough without your dreams fulfilled, there comes a sad twist. The twist comes when your dreams are all you have left because it is too disappointing to live in the reality that your mate is unable to love you. One spouse explained it like this: "Living for years with my unemotional mate had caused me to think that there must be something wrong with me. That my need for love was wrong, that no one could fill it. I felt I should give up my desire for an intimate relationship because my husband didn't think it was important. I began to wonder why I should try so hard to get someone to love me. I seemed to be the only one starving for love so it must be my unfulfilled need, not my husband's obligation to fill me or make me feel loved. Or at least that is what I've told myself, not realizing it is his emotionless way of life that has contributed to my emotional hunger and confusion."

NOT TRUE TO YOURSELF

This book will focus on what happens when you live with a mate that is either unavailable to meet your emotional needs (emotionally unavailable) or unable to communicate positive, tender emotions (unemotional). These are considered very common and subtle forms of disrespect that have often been misunderstood and are devastating problems that can be hard to identify. Most of the time, the unemotional mate is unaware of his or her lack of emotions, which leaves the other mate struggling to get emotional needs met. When you live without the opportunity to communicate what is in your heart and mind, you will not feel loved, respected, and accepted. If you feel trapped or unable to change your situation, you can eventually believe your only choices are to resign yourself to live in a loveless, unsatisfying relationship or decide to become one more divorce statistic.

You are not true to yourself if you believe for one minute you must exist in a relationship without love or emotions. When you only *exist* in a relationship, you become physically, spiritually, and emotionally unfaithful to yourself, the relationship, and to God. You are not true to what you want and need, not true to what God wants or needs from you, not true to what your mate wants or needs from you, and not living up to what your children deserve from you! You may believe you are having a loving and satisfying relationship, despite the loneliness you feel. Unfortunately, you probably are not fully aware of what the truth is for your life. Like so many others, you may not know what a meaningful, loving, satisfying, and close relationship looks or feels like. As a result, you *settle* for living with less of a relationship than what you really deserve.

I could see the hurt in Mary's eyes as she continued with her story. "Why have I allowed myself to live in this relationship without love?" Mary said with regret and sadness in her voice. She had never realized her loneliness and not feeling loved was a result of Phil's emotional unavailability. She never realized that she was being disrespected when Phil discouraged her and other family members from expressing feelings. Until now, Mary never understood that Phil was unemotional or that she was living in an emotionless relationship. To this point, Mary always thought the lack of emotions and loneliness was a normal part of life. Mary has come to understand that emotions and love are what should be normal in her relationship. She was delighted to learn it was not too late to change how she felt inside and change how she related to Phil.

WITHOUT EMOTIONS YOU WILL NOT HAVE A LOVING RELATIONSHIP

Without expressing emotions you will not have the ability to establish or maintain a meaningful relationship with love and respect. "What is a meaningful relationship?" you may ask. It's when you can express what is inside your heart or mind and just be yourself without being afraid of rejection. It's when you can freely share thoughts, dreams, sorrows, and tears, believing they are accepted and respected without question. It's when you feel safe, secure, and loved inside your heart, like being wrapped in a warm, cozy blanket on a cold winter's night. Those feelings shared from one heart to another are the very interactions that generate a sense of personal acceptance, worth, and importance that goes beyond ordinary lip service.

Mary's heartache is one of the most common consequences of an emotionless relationship. When your thoughts and feelings are not allowed or accepted, you do not feel loved or respected as a person and you begin to question your own self-worth. How worthy you feel about yourself is often related to how your feelings are received from the important people in your life. The relationship can blossom or be shattered by your partner's response to the emotions you express.

Like Mary, you may desire love, acceptance, and meaningful conversation. The feelings generated by the burdens and treasured moments in your life are meant to be shared, not hidden away where they lose their meaning. Having a tender moment happen in your life is only half the significance. *Sharing* the tender moment is the other half. Sharing life's difficulties with someone is how burdens become lighter and healing takes place. There is a verse in the Bible that says, "Two are better than one, because they have a good return for their work: If one falls down, his friend can help him up. But pity the man who falls and has no one to help him up!" (Ecclesiastes 4:9–10). Sharing what is in your heart lifts the heaviness and brings encouragement to the soul to carry you through to fight the next battle. If you are unable to experience what you feel and think within your heart and mind, you will struggle to feel loved and respected in any relationship, even in your relationship with God.

WHEN THERE IS NO EMOTION, THERE IS NO AFFECTION

Signs of affection such as tender hugs, kisses, and touches are all outward expressions of inward emotions. Unfortunately, a life without emotion creates relationships without affection. The unemotional mate lacks the ability to give affection because they do not have the emotion to give, and there is not an understanding why affection is important to make a person feel loved. The lack of affection from an unemotional mate inevitably creates distance within the relationship, eroding the emotional union and destroying any potential for emotional growth as a couple. Additionally, lack of affection has long-lasting, devastating effects on the emotional well-being of current family members and those in future generations. Being in a relationship without emotion and affection is a lonely and agonizing way to live. Meaningful relationships are based on foundational needs such as being loved, accepted, respected, and appreciated. How you express those needs to one another will greatly influence the success or destruction of the relationship.

WORDS OF ENCOURAGEMENT

Are you living in a relationship like Mary and Phil? Have your dreams and needs been crushed? Are you struggling in a relationship that lacks emotions, love, and respect? Have you been waiting for your relationship to change, trying everything you can think of, only to be continually disappointed, disrespected, and unloved? The purpose of this book is to provide radical solutions to both the unemotional mate and the emotional mate in order to make drastic changes in the relationship. Hang on to your seat, because you will be surprised by what you learn and what you will be expected to change to make your needs, wants, and prayers come true.

≈

STUDY QUESTIONS

1. Describe how you or someone you know is living a relationship similar to Mary and Phil.

2. What were your dreams and prayers for your relationship with your mate and what has been the reality of your situation?

3. Describe what a "meaningful and close relationship" means to you and how you have been struggling to obtain love and respect with your mate.

2

WHEN YOU LIVE
WITHOUT EMOTIONS

~

*The best and most beautiful things in the
world cannot be seen or even touched. They
must be felt within the heart.*
Helen Keller

Elliot was a successful corporate lawyer.[1] Life was going
very well until he was suddenly diagnosed with a brain tumor
the size of a small orange. Choosing to live, Elliot decided to
undergo surgery to remove the tumor. The surgery was considered a success and Elliot eventually returned to work with
much of the same intellectual ability as before. It wasn't long,
however, before people began to recognize that there seemed
to be a change in his personality. Elliot was not using his time
wisely; he was becoming upset over minor details and was
showing little sense of responsibility for his actions. Along
with these behavior changes, a succession of life alterations
took place: his wife left him, he wasted away his savings, and
he was fired from his job.

Wondering what caused these problems, Elliot underwent
extensive testing that concluded there was nothing wrong with
his thinking. Seeking further help, Elliot consulted a neurologist who also found nothing wrong with his logic, memory,
or attention. However, something the neurologist noticed
was very striking. During the entire time they discussed the

traumatic events of his life, Elliot displayed no emotion regarding the things that happened. As Elliot told his personal, horrific, and life-changing story there was no hint of regret, sadness, frustration, anger, or emotional pain. The neurologist concluded that the combination of the brain tumor and the surgical removal of part of the prefrontal lobes had severed the ties between the emotional part of Elliot's brain and the thinking abilities of his brain. Elliot was able to make computer-like decisions, but unable to assign values to differing issues in life. Every decision was neutral. The doctor found that Elliot's difficulty with making decisions was directly connected to his inability to have feelings.

In his book, *Emotional Intelligence,* psychologist Daniel Goleman emphasizes that, "One lesson from Elliot's indecisiveness is the crucial role of feeling in navigating the endless stream of life's personal decisions. While strong feelings can create havoc in reasoning, the lack of awareness of feeling can also be ruinous, especially in weighing the decisions on which our destiny largely depends: what career to pursue, whether to stay with a secure job or switch to one that is riskier but more interesting, whom to date or marry, where to live . . . Such decisions cannot be made well through sheer rationality; they require gut feeling, and the emotional wisdom garnered through past experiences. Formal logic alone can never work as the basis for deciding who to marry or trust or even what job to take; these are realms where reason without feeling is blind."[2]

LIVING WITHOUT EMOTIONS

Elliot's story is not meant to make you race to your doctor to find out if your unemotional mate ever had surgery. It is to emphasize that feelings play a vital part in making personal decisions. Telling others your innermost desires, needs, and reactions, regarding what is happening, are how you let those feelings out. Living an unemotional life similar to Elliot is like living in a glass bubble that surrounds your very being. You can see and hear everything, but it's as if you are in your own secluded world. You don't let people into your world, and you have a difficult time reaching out. Even the people that matter the most (or should matter the most) have a hard time penetrating that bubble. You can see them, but there is always something that separates you. That is why you struggle with relationships, even with God. The unemotional person believes emotions are not important since they can make you weak, get in the way of logical thinking, and/or threaten your control on life. In fact, this is how the unemotional person expects everyone else to be. This way of thinking is subtle, socially acceptable, and very damaging for relationships.

CHARACTERISTICS OF A PERSON THAT IS UNEMOTIONAL

As I mentioned in the preface, the characteristics for the emotionally unavailable or unemotional individual are very similar in nature. Although the emotionally unavailable mate may show some negative emotions, such as anger, both individuals have difficulty showing healthy emotions and are unable to provide healthy encouragement or support when emotions are expressed by others. A person that is emotionally unavailable or unemotional will fit many of the following characteristics. (These characteristics will be explained in detail throughout the book using the term "unemotional mate.")

- Has (or had) people and experiences in life that have discouraged emotions
- Stubborn and sees life more in extremes—black and white

- Relates more with facts and logic rather than with emotions of the heart
- Unable to emotionally respond and validate the feelings of others
- Rarely shows emotion (crying) or initiates physical signs of tenderness (hugs or kisses)
- Does not understand why others show emotions and believe it is a sign of weakness
- Tunes people out when emotions are being expressed
- Struggles with getting emotionally close to people, including God
- Has difficulty with conversations that include feelings about self or others
- Demonstrates love by performing tasks or giving material "things" rather than by showing signs of love and tenderness
- If physical affection is given, there is an expectation to receive a favor in return
- Believes sex is what makes you emotionally close, rather than feeling close from a loving relationship—or emotions are so closed there is no desire for sex.

HOW THE UNEMOTIONAL PERSON RELATES WITH OTHERS

When emotions are not part of your life, you will struggle with relating to people and situations of daily living. Since unemotional people do not know how to deal with emotions the person will use a variety of ways to handle daily circumstances. For the unemotional person, the following behaviors can become the normal way of handling life. But, to others (especially family members), the behaviors can be seen as very frustrating, disappointing, irrational, childish, defiant, and irresponsible.

Just the facts

Since emotions are not part of life, unemotional people relate through facts, logic, and rules. If someone is hurt, showing compassion, tenderness, and empathy rarely happens since they do not have the capacity to use feelings to connect with the heart. Discussions will center on what and why something happened rather than a sensitive conversation to understand how the person feels or how they are dealing with the issues. When you don't have emotions, there is not the capability to show affection, love, and tenderness to encourage a trusting, close relationship and little ability to validate or encourage emotions in others.

Matt was successful at his job and his strong work ethic made him serious about getting the job done right with little time for idle chitchat. If a fellow employee showed some emotion over an issue, Matt would become irritated inside. Matt might listen and offer some advice, but what he really wanted was to tell the person, "Quit your moaning and get back to work." Matt could get away with his insensitive nature at work since his productivity thrived on his unemotional state of mind. However, his emotional insensitivity was very evident with his lack of patience and inability to get emotionally close with his wife and children. How Matt treated others was very frustrating, disheartening, and disappointing to his family members.

If you ignore it long enough, it will go away

Tom was raised in a family that did not deal well with conflict. His parents did not follow through with solving sensitive issues. They often "swept things under the rug" believing that if they ignored the problems they would just go away.

These behaviors became so common for Tom that he continued them into adulthood. Tom would put off making decisions and often ignore sensitive issues, hoping the problem would go away on its own. Of course, the problem just got worse and his wife's constant reminder about the issue only made Tom want to ignore it even more. Because of Tom's behavior his wife handled many of the decisions that made her feel even more aggravated and resentful. She interpreted his ignoring things as if he didn't care and didn't love her. In reality, Tom's ignoring and indecision came from fear of conflict, poor self-esteem, laziness, and the learned behaviors of his parents.

Tuning out

Joe has an incredible ability to tune everybody and everything out of his life by watching television, reading the paper, working on the computer, or working in the garage. This is particularly aggravating to his wife, Sara, who feels they can never communicate because Joe is in his own little world. "I feel like I'm invisible; I might as well talk to the wall," complained Sara. When Joe was a child, there was so much chaos at home he quickly learned to escape from it by watching television. "There was so much going on in my house growing up," Joe shared, "I would sit in front of the TV and tune out my parents' arguments." Like Joe, children that live in hurtful, unemotional, or chaotic homes survive by withdrawing into their own world or through activities to block out the chaos and hurt. Some children escape into excessive amounts of reading, computer games, playing outside, daydreaming, or playing in their bedroom. Whatever survival behaviors worked during childhood, the same type of behaviors will likely continue in adulthood.

Shutting down

Molly would not express much emotion when she was disappointed or hurt. In fact, she would not do much of anything. Molly grew up in a home where emotions were discouraged and not expressed. When she cried, disagreed, or became angry, she was either sent to her room or told statements such as, "Stop acting like a baby." Molly came to believe early in life that emotions were wrong and that she needed to shut off her feelings to keep the peace in her home. As an adult, whenever Molly did not express herself, her husband would interpret her silence as if she didn't care or that she didn't love him. Similar to Molly, when a person reacts through silence or shutting down, it destroys any chance of communication and leaves the mate feeling aggravated, misunderstood, and lonely.

Walking away

Todd has never liked conflict. Even small arguments with his wife would make him feel uncomfortable enough that he wanted to leave. He never realized that the childhood experience of witnessing arguments between his family members would affect him this much. He had to search hard and deep to remember how uncomfortable he felt when his parents started to argue. He realized his parents' arguing was why he played outside to get away from the turmoil. As an adult, Todd's dislike of conflict triggered his need to get away. "I feel abandoned every time he leaves," his wife said, "like he doesn't care about me." For the spouse experiencing a mate walking away, it is especially hurtful. Not only is your partner ignoring you, you also get a second slap in the face when you feel physically abandoned. This is devastating to any relationship.

Bursting out

The longer an unemotional person holds in emotions, the greater the likelihood those emotions will burst out to relieve the growing tension. Since unemotional people do not know how to express themselves appropriately, there will often be an accumulation of emotions just waiting to be released. The release can come through anger and yelling or in the form of behaviors such as emotional temper tantrums, whining, stomping around, slamming doors, throwing things, driving fast, threats to themselves or others, and senseless arguments. Suppressed anger can also show through physical outbursts like hitting, shoving, and physical fighting. This type of behavior can be very hurtful and destructive to other members of the family. Often the family members become confused as to why they bear the brunt of these hurtful outbursts. Such hurtful behaviors cut deep to the core, destroying any connection of trust or respect in the family relationships.

WHY DON'T YOU CHANGE?

I have often been asked questions like: "Why can't they change?" "Why would an adult continue these same immature behaviors into adulthood?" "Why doesn't the person know they are acting this way?"

Often, these behaviors were learned during the early years in life, as a way to survive what was happening. As an innocent child, you simply responded to the hurtful or chaotic childhood situations the best way you knew how. If no one taught you differently (and especially if you continue to live in hurtful and chaotic situations), you would continue with the same behaviors and not realize your behaviors are inappropriate or immature. People remain immature because they are emotionally stuck at an early age when they were originally hurt. Since immature people do not like to be corrected by others, it is very difficult to talk to that person about their inappropriate behaviors. A person has a better chance to change inappropriate behaviors when the childhood hurts that started the behaviors, become healed.

WORDS OF ENCOURAGEMENT

Whether you are the unemotional mate or the partner that lives with the unemotional mate, you are not alone in your struggles. You *can* make changes as long as you choose to change. One of the purposes of this book is to help you find answers as to why the unemotional person has difficulty expressing emotions and to learn new ways to emotionally relate with thoughts and feelings. You need to know that God did not create relationships to be without emotions. However, if you want your situation to change, you must start taking responsibility for the way you *have* been responding to your mate and take responsibility to learn how to respond differently. This will be explained in the chapter to come. Keep reading!

Personal Reflection

May I accept help to open my eyes to what I need to see; open my ears to what I need to hear; and open my heart to what I need to feel.

≈

STUDY QUESTIONS

1. How do you or someone you know fit the characteristics described above?

2. Describe how you or someone you know has handled life in the ways listed above?

3. After reading this chapter, what additional insights have you learned about yourself, and what can you do to change your life for the better?

3

LIVING IN A FAMILY WITHOUT EMOTIONS

~

When you live in a black and white world,
you cannot see the rainbows in life.

Mel saw himself as a good husband and provider for the family. He worked long hours and was not home very much, which added to the feelings of loneliness that his wife, Jenny, felt from Mel not being emotionally available. As much as Jenny tried to ask Mel to show her more love and attention, he would be too busy or give some excuse. Jenny resigned herself a long time ago to give up trying to get more love from Mel. Since Mel was a good provider, Jenny wondered if she had a right to complain about her situation. To get through the day, Jenny would often put aside those thoughts and focus her energy on trying to be the best mom she could be to the kids.

Mel saw his rules and discipline for the home as a source of love and security because he did not know how to give love through a compassionate, heartfelt relationship. The girls loved their dad and wanted to do what he said, but his stern approach had always made it difficult to talk with him, which put a big strain on their relationships. Because of the emotional distance Mel felt with his girls, he believed the rules would keep the girls safer and bring a closer relationship with his daughters. "I'm only doing this because I love them," he would often say. Over the years, the girls felt dad's rules were too restrictive and his enforcement of the rules came with a heavy price. The girls gave in to dad's demands because there was no talking to him about it, and they knew they would never win.

These rules would be the fuel that ignited the arguments between Mel and Jenny. The girls would often go to Jenny to argue their point whenever Mel lowered the hammer on anyone's request to bend the rules. This usually disappointed and hurt the girls since they felt they could not freely express feelings or share what was on their mind. Jenny could see how the girls were hurt when Mel would tell them to go to their room when they were upset or going to cry. When Mel blamed Jenny for interfering with his discipline, he would make subtle little digs that would be hurtful to Jenny. When Jenny tried to stand up to his unjust comments or extreme discipline, Mel would make stinging comments that were like verbal bullets that penetrated Jenny's heart. As a result, Jenny would back down, shutting off her thoughts and emotions.

Over the years the girls and Jenny tucked their feelings inside, not realizing the devastating toll each cutting word, disappointment, or hurt had on their heart and soul. What you need to understand is that Mel was accustomed to the unemotional, strict life that he forced on everyone else. However, Mel's emotionless living was like a cancerous tumor, hidden inside, internally destroying any resemblance of a loving, compassionate family relationship. The years of emotionless living had shut down Jenny's heart long ago and conditioned the girls' hearts to expect it in future relationships.

RULES AND LOGIC VS. RELATIONSHIP AND EMOTION

If you live in a situation similar to Mel and his family, there is always this underlying caution or emotional distance with the unemotional person. When a family member is angered by the strict rules or hurt by the lack of tenderness, the unemotional person shows little sensitivity. The comments (or silence) from the unemotional person ultimately makes others feel they are wrong to express feelings or give an opinion. This way of treating people usually becomes the "normal" way of living for the unemotional person, which reinforces the belief he or she is always right. This belief hinders the unemotional person's ability to see how they hurt others, even if someone points it out. This treatment destroys the foundation of a relationship. When emotions are not part of a person's life, similar to Mel, you relate more through rules and logic rather than a relationship. If someone is hurt, showing compassion, tenderness, and empathy rarely happens since he does not have the capacity to use feelings to connect with the other person. Discussions will center on the facts of what and why something happened rather than a sensitive conversation to understand how the person is feeling or dealing with the problem. When you are unemotional, giving out rules and discussing the facts becomes your way to relate, rather than showing affection and compassion as a way to encourage a trusting relationship. The more others follow your rules and talk about facts, the more you believe you have a close relationship.

FORCED RESPECT VS. LOVING RESPECT

In a home like Mel and Jenny, the family members are *expected* to comply with the rules, through performance and consequences rather than working through issues together with acceptance and compromise. This is the difference between what I call *forced respect* and *loving respect*. *Forced respect* is when the unemotional mate expects (or demands) other family members to comply with rules and verbal commands or else face the consequences. Because there is no emotional connection in the relationship, the unemotional mate believes there is a relationship when the family member complies with the rules or commands. When the daughters complied with his rules, Mel believed he had a good relationship with them. However, the strict rules only created more distance and fear between Mel and the other family members.

On the other hand, *loving respect* is when you first have a loving relationship with the family members and they comply because of the love, acceptance, and respect they receive in the relationship. With loving respect, you are given far more love than you are given rules or discipline. As a result, even if your relationship includes discipline, such as, timeouts, limits, groundings, etc., you do not feel as hurt because you already know deep inside that the discipline is done out of love. You see, forced respect is based on rules which force someone to comply out of fear. Where loving respect is based on loving someone to the point they will be motivated to comply because they feel loved and do not want to disappoint you.

LIVING IN A BLACK AND WHITE WORLD

Living in a world of black and white is typically a by-product of a childhood that consists of hurtful, compassion-less, restrictive, and/or abusive caregivers and experiences. It can also come from growing up in a home with rigid rules or strict religion with little praise and love. The more you interpret the world in black and white, the more dependent you are on rules and facts to help you relate with others. You will rarely let your guard down and you are determined to be right about everything, lacking humility in the process. You hurt others by either not talking to them or being brutally honest with them. The more you interpret the world in black and white, the less room there is for negotiations or compromise, with no emotion involved in the decision-making process. If someone disagrees with you, your argument will leave little opportunity for discussion. In other words, people cannot win with extreme black-and-white thinkers. Everything is, "right or wrong," "yes or no," or "my way or no way."

This narrow-mindedness is often seen in positions of high responsibility or authority. As a result, the status of your position and/or knowledge allows justification of your hard-line stance since you cannot relate any other way. If you are a religious black-and-white thinker, you may utilize your status and your knowledge of scriptures as a weapon to get a point across. For example, when someone disagrees or has an opposite opinion, the black-and-white thinker would have little discussion except to respond with a scripture to prove you wrong. Even if you had a correct and valid point of concern, you are made to feel you are wrong to express your feelings or opinions, while you leave feeling worse than when you entered the conversation.

As a black-and-white thinker, you are blinded from seeing your own extreme thinking and strongly justify your position because you do not like to be corrected. You need to know where you stand on every issue of life because you do not want to be wrong or caught off guard with any decision. This way of thinking also creates the need to control people and situations because you would never want to be left without knowing what is going on.

FILLING EMOTIONAL EMPTINESS

If you are like Jenny or the daughters, you may be living in the same type of house, feeling alone and shut out from any sense of meaningful relationship. Because of this, you become frustrated and disappointed from your repeated failures to have any significant interaction with the unemotional person and the chance to fulfill your dream of a loving relationship and close family. In order to survive, you resign yourself to the family struggles and squelch your feelings by consuming yourself with other activities. When there is no satisfaction from your relationships at home, the desire to fill the emotional emptiness is what lures family members to find meaning in other areas of life. When you pursue other activities outside the family, those activities become your substitute for what a meaningful relationship should be accomplishing.

For example, you may spend more time away from the family or specifically away from the unemotional mate in activities such as: work, religion, reading, other relationships, telephone conversations, sleeping, child care, internet surfing, computer games, shopping, television viewing, and recreational sports. These are the most common, accessible, and justifiable alternatives to relationship fulfillment since these activities are usually already in your life. When these pursuits become excessive, there is a decay of the emotional, physical, and spiritual union with the spouse and family. The warning signs that your pursuits are becoming unhealthy are when you become excessively consumed in other pursuits to the exclusion of spending time with your mate or family. It is often the case when family members are feeling an excessive amount of loneliness, hurt, anger, or fear from the home situation; they feel justified in spending excessive amounts of time in these activities. This will be discussed in more detail later in the book.

WORDS OF ENCOURAGEMENT

Are you are living in a world with more rules than a relationship? Are you living in a world that is black and white, unable to see the many colors of life? As common as it may be for you to live this way, you probably are not finding much fulfillment in life. You can make the decision to change how you live. However, you must acknowledge that you are living by rules or a black and white life and identify how this is affecting you. As you begin to realize the seriousness of what is happening, you can make the choice to change how you are living and responding to others. As difficult as it may be to realize this about your life, don't give up! There are ways to change! Continue reading to learn what to do next.

Personal Reflection

*May I accept help to see the rules
that destroy the relationships in my life,
and may I see what I can do to bring
life into those relationships.*

STUDY QUESTIONS

1. Describe how you or someone you know has been affected like Mel, Jenny, or the daughters in the following areas:
   a. Living in a home with an unemotional person.
   b. Living in a home with black and white thinking.
   c. Living in a home with excessive rules.

2. Describe how you may be filling the emotional emptiness with other pursuits.

3. After reading this chapter, what additional insights have you learned about yourself and what can you do to change your life for the better?

4

PAST EXPERIENCES ARE THE GREATEST INFLUENCE

~

The more hurt you hold in from your past,
the more you will hurt in the future.

Unemotional people tend to be the biggest skeptics when it comes to believing how the past can influence their lives. What is most revealing and interesting, however, is how early in life you can be affected. With the advancement of research over the years, there is increasing evidence demonstrating how the early stages of life can be influential on all aspects of human awareness, senses, and the influence on your ability to live a meaningful life. In the article, *Mysteries of Prenatal Consciousness,* Sarah Belle Dougherty enlightens us with the following revelations. "We now know that the unborn child is an aware, reacting human being who from the sixth month on (and perhaps even earlier) leads an active emotional life. Along with this startling finding we have made these discoveries: 'The fetus can see, hear, experience, taste and, on a primitive level, even learn in utero . . . Most importantly, he can feel—not with an adult's sophistication, but feel nonetheless."[3] Ms. Dougherty is even more direct when she writes, "From the 24th week on he hears all the time—listening to the noises in his mother's body, and to voices, music, etc."[4]

In his book, *The Secret Life of the Unborn Child,* Dr. Thomas Verny indicates that the unborn child is a feeling, remembering, and aware little being. He writes, "At first, he [the embryo] can only do simple emotional equations. As his memory and experience expand, he gradually acquires the ability to make more discriminating and subtle connections. By birth, however, the infant is mature enough to be able to respond to maternal feelings with great accuracy and compose physical, emotional and cognitive responses."[5] As a result, the mother and father's attitude through feelings and behaviors of love, acceptance, and positive thoughts for the fetus creates the foundation for what the child will imitate in their life after birth. Dr. Verny is very direct when he writes, "If loving nurturing mothers bear more self-confident, secure children, it is because the self-aware 'I' of each infant is carved out of warmth and love. Similarly, if unhappy, depressed or ambivalent mothers bear a higher rate of neurotic children, it is because their offsprings' egos were molded in moments of dread and anguish. Not surprisingly, without redirection, such children often grow into suspicious, anxious and emotionally fragile adults."[6]

He further informs us that, "The second most important prenatal influence is the father's attitude toward the pregnancy and his commitment to the relationship with the mother. One investigator has estimated from his studies that women trapped in a stormy marriage run 'a 237 percent greater risk of bearing a psychologically or physically damaged child than a woman in a secure, nurturing relationship.'"[7] This research is startling concerning how early we begin our emotional journey and how powerful the primary people in our life affect our emotions and our future.

EARLY EXPERIENCES SHAPE YOUR EXPRESSIONS

There should be no doubt that you are born with the ability to express the full spectrum of emotions that God created within you. However, you may ask, "If God created everyone with emotions, how does a person get to the point of living without the ability to express them?" That is the very point you need to grasp. It was the early experiences with the important people in your life (parents, extended family, teachers, pastors, and friends) that encouraged or discouraged how you would express your thoughts and feelings. Those experiences also shaped what you believed was important in life, how you acted toward life, and how you will express yourself the rest of your life.

In my first book, *When Feelings Don't Come Easy,* I mention that your life was molded by the ability of the caregivers to meet your needs of safety, trust, nurturing, love, and acceptance. When you were a young and innocent child the world was like a new kindergarten classroom full of exciting sights, sounds, and adventures. At that young age, the experiences stirred up fear, tears, laughter, or whatever type of physical or emotional response the circumstances would trigger. God intended your responses to be an automatic natural reflex, like taking your next breath. God created you to react with laughter when something tickled your funny bone or to express tears when something hurt you.[8] Those early experiences will build the emotional foundation from which you will base how to express feelings in the future.

While Donna sat quietly in my office, you could see the sadness in her face from the years of emptiness in her life. She couldn't explain why she felt a distance between herself and everyone she wanted to be close with. Even with the people she considered friends, there seemed to be an invisible wall that would go up that kept everyone out. She never understood why it was difficult to become emotionally close to people. Exploring her childhood, Donna was not allowed to talk about feelings. Emotions were only seen in the form of parents yelling, which made getting close to her mother difficult. Whenever Donna tried to warm up to her mother, something would set her mother off like a skyrocket. Donna would find herself getting hurt over and over again, until that desire to get close withered away—like something died between them. Looking back, Donna visualized a disappointed and frightened little girl. As she kept emotions inside, pushing herself away from her mother was the safest thing to do. Donna began to understand how the fear and disappointments from her earliest relationships had followed her into adulthood and kept her from getting close to others.

THE PAST AFFECTS YOUR RELATIONSHIPS

Your perception of how to relate and express feelings in a relationship is usually based on the observations and experiences from the significant relationships early in your life. *In essence, your ability to develop meaningful relationships as an adult has everything to do with how meaningful your relationships were with the adults in your childhood and teenage years.* How those significant people in your life related to you became your role model to teach you how you are to relate with others. For example, during the years growing up, when you were hurt, angry, sad, or disappointed, were you able to safely and freely express your feelings with others? Did you receive a hug when you needed comfort for your hurts? If the answer is no to these questions, then ask yourself, "Does the same thing happen now?" Can you freely express your hurts, sadness, disappointments, and anger with your mate? Do you allow others to safely and freely express their feelings? Do you emotionally relate any better with your mate or children than you did with the relationships in your childhood? The good news is that you now have a choice to be different and foster better relationships. However, that choice is up to you. You will find more about improving your relationships later in the book.

STRUGGLING WITH YOUR RELATIONSHIP WITH GOD

You may have struggled in the area of relationships for so long, you don't recognize how shallow or unhealthy your relationships have become. This is also true for a relationship with God. If you have not experienced trusting, open, and secure relationships, you would not know how to trust or feel secure with God. In fact, your ability to have a relationship with God has everything to do with the type of relationship you had with caregivers early in your life. Those early relationship experiences were also the role model for what you will expect with God. For example, if your parents were there for you when you were hurt, encouraging you and loving you no matter what happened, those early experiences created a strong belief in your mind and a strong belief (faith) that someone cared. As a result, you will carry the belief and faith into your relationship with God. Learning how to have a trusting relationship is born out of the loving, caring relationships that you experience early in life. Learning to have faith in God is created from the early relationships that were faithful in loving you no matter what.

However, if you could not count on your parents to be there during thick and thin, you will more likely struggle to count on God to be there for you, especially when the storms of life are rough. If your parents were not physically or emotionally available, it becomes even more difficult to believe in a relationship you cannot see or touch. This may cause you to struggle with your belief in God's existence and your faith may waver with the problems you face. The good news is you can learn to have love, trust, and faith in God as you pray to receive it into your heart. If you struggle with your relationship with God, He wants you to tell Him about your struggles. Let Him know you want a relationship and stand on what the Word of God says. "May our Lord Jesus Christ himself and God our Father, who loved us and by his grace gave us eternal encouragement and good hope, encourage your hearts and strengthen you in every good deed and word," (2 Thessalonians 2:16,17).

INFLUENCING THE NEXT GENERATION

Your parents' decision to treat you the way they did was from what they learned from the generation before them. If you are living in a home that does not share emotions and does not show signs of love or words of praises, that is what you are teaching your children. How you treat your children (the next generation) is also a choice that only you have control over. This is evident in the Bible verse Jeremiah 32:18 stating that God allows, "the punishment for the fathers' sins into the laps of their children after them. O great and powerful God, whose name is the Lord Almighty." In other words, God gives everyone the choice whether to pass on the hurts to their children after them. But God also wants you to have the best relationship with your family now and for the generations after you. For example, if the dad in the house is unemotional, chances are the sons will not learn how to express themselves and the daughters will look for someone to marry just like the dad. If the mother in the house does not express her opinion or feelings, chances are the daughters will not learn how to express themselves and the sons will look for someone to marry just like mom. What legacy do you want to pass on to the next generation? There is always the ability to make changes in the next generation as long as you begin to make changes in your own life. Ultimately, it is up to you to start making the changes where you are now.

WORDS OF ENCOURAGEMENT

God never intended anyone to live an emotionless life, especially when feelings are a part of your creation. Feelings are supposed to be expressed like taking your next breath. Somewhere along the way, your ability to express yourself was never learned or encouraged. Your circumstances and relationships through life greatly influence how you relate to others. If your past was something you would like to put behind you, take heart! The good news is, regardless of what has happened in your past, it does NOT determine your future if you make the decision to be different. You have the choice to make your future different from your past.

Personal Reflection
May I accept the help to let go of those things
that were in the past so I can enjoy the present
and look forward to the future.

≈

STUDY QUESTIONS

The more you can learn about the relationships in your past, the more you can use that information to improve the relationships you have in the present. You can answer these questions on your own or take turns answering the following questions with your mate. If you do not remember much of the past, talk with a family member to learn about your family.

- Describe your mother (and/or stepmother)
    1. How did she show sadness, anger, fear and joy to you and other family members?

2. How were you able to communicate thoughts and feelings?
3. How did (or didn't) she show feelings of love, caring or acceptance (i.e., were you hugged, kissed, told you were loved)?
4. How did (or didn't) she discipline you?
5. Did she have any good or bad habits/attitudes that influence the family?

- Describe your father (and/or stepfather): Repeat above questions 1 to 5

- Describe other significant relationships in your past (grandparents, aunts, uncles, teachers): Repeat above questions 1 to 5

- How did (or didn't) your parents show affection (hugging/kissing/caring words) toward each other?

- How did your parents deal with making decisions for the family?

- How did your parents deal with disagreements and conflict?

- Describe any significant events that negatively influenced your important relationships (divorce, separation, death, etc.). How did those events affect you emotionally?

- Using the above answers, discuss with your mate how the past relationships influenced the behaviors and expression of feelings you now have in your relationships as an adult?

Have each mate answer these questions:

1. How do you communicate anger, sadness, fear and joy to the family?

2. How do you accept words or actions of affection and love from others?

3. How do you give words or actions of affection and love to others?

4. How do you allow decisions to be made in the family?

5. How do you react to different family members when there are disagreements or conflict?

6. Are you able to get emotionally close (freely give and receive hugs, kisses, say, "I love you") to the important people in your life?

7. What are the similarities and differences between your past relationships and how you react, think, and feel in the relationships you have now as an adult?

PART II

when emotions don't come easy in relationships

5

WHY YOU LIVE WITH AN UNEMOTIONAL MATE

~

*You will accept love only after
you feel worthy enough to receive it.*

L iving with an unemotional mate can be one of the most difficult challenges of your life. As one woman said, "Living with my husband is like living in two different worlds." Another said, "It's worse than living in a prison or taking care of another child." No matter how much you try to speak to your mate, it's like you're speaking a foreign language. If you live this way long enough you become numb to the disappointment of not having your dream of a loving, affectionate mate that will care for you and the family. You may have struggled alone to keep the marriage alive and the family members together only to become frustrated for allowing yourself to live that way. You may have pondered why you are living with someone who has not fulfilled your emotional needs. You wonder why you have worked so hard to make the relationship work with little to show for it and have difficulty feeling emotionally close to your mate, friends, even God. In this chapter, I will explain the characteristics of a person who lives with an unemotional mate.

Since you grew up in a home where you did not experience trusting, close relationships with one or both of your caregivers, you struggle with developing and maintaining trusting, close relationships with others.

The greatest influence to your feeling loved was through the quality of relationships you witnessed and experienced with the people that mattered the most in your childhood and teen years. As you grew up in a home without experiencing emotionally close relationships, you were accustomed to lack of love and lack of attention. This sets the stage for the type of relationship you would be accustomed to living throughout your life. In addition, you have great difficulty (although you may not think so) with trusting others and maintaining long-term close relationships. People who struggle with getting close build walls to keep people at a safe distance. There will be more details about this in the chapter, "Dancing the Relationship Tango."

You are willing to work harder, wait longer, and do whatever it takes in order to receive love and attention from your unemotional mate.

As a child you would desire a loving, caring, close relationship with your parents. However, if your parents were emotionally or physically unavailable, you may have taken on the responsibility to establish the emotional connection that your parents should have initiated. If the situation did not change, your innocent mind would take the blame for the relationship failure, which would motivate you to work harder to receive the love you wanted. As you establish relationships in adulthood the same dilemma would happen by unknowingly finding a mate that is emotionally or physically unavailable. Since you would not want your relationship to end as another failure, you would again fall into the same situation, believing you need to work harder to fix the relationship. Since you have worked to fix relationships all your life, working harder, waiting longer, and doing whatever it takes to make the relationship work becomes a normal pattern of life.

Since you did not receive affection growing up, you have a greater chance of becoming uncomfortable with affection when you receive it in adulthood.

If you grew up in a home where one or both caregivers did not provide affection (frequent hugs, kisses, tender touches, words of love and praise), you do not know what heartfelt, tender affection looks or feels like. As a result, you may be more accustomed to a relationship based on surface love, such as being a good provider of your material, social, and financial needs. You are more accustomed to the absence of affection in a relationship than you are with receiving affection. For example, when you are with someone significant (boy/girl friend or spouse), you may feel "uncomfortable," "smothered," "closed in," "trapped," or "wanting space" when you spend too much "good" time with them or you get too close. You desire affection and become disappointed when your mate does not give it, but you have a hard time accepting it when it comes your way. This will be discussed in more detail later in the book.

You put others first, to the point of excluding your own needs and feelings.

If you lived or live in relationships that are hurtful or unemotional, you are more accustomed to people that disrespect you than give you love, encouragement, and appreciation. You have a tendency to believe you must work harder at everything in order to win acceptance and prove your worthiness. Unfortunately, the ungrateful, disrespectful, or unemotional response you receive from the other person perpetuates the same belief that your work is not acceptable. As a result, you will always consider the needs of others (at the exclusion of your own) in order to accomplish the task of winning their approval and feeling better about yourself.

One area of confusion that typically comes with putting

others first is where you draw the line between Christian servanthood and giving too much of yourself. During the three years Jesus was in ministry, He gave of Himself by ministering to others through prayer, healing, and preaching. However, Jesus also was aware of His own human physical and emotional limitations and the need to take care of Himself. For example, while ministering to people, Jesus would leave the crowd (even with people still needing help) to find rest and spend some time alone with His Heavenly Father. What about you? Do you give yourself time to get away to refresh your mind, body, and soul? Like Jesus, give yourself permission to have a break from the demands of your husband, children, job, and the church. If you do not recharge your heart, mind, and soul, you will not be as effective in helping others.

You are willing to endure more insults and less respect because of one or more of the following:

1. When you received negative comments, insults, and disrespect in the past you are more likely to accept it as normal and endure it in the future.

2. When you are hurting inside from the past, you are more likely to let others continue to hurt you.

3. When you don't feel good about yourself, you believe you deserve insults and you are willing to accept disrespect from others.

4. Because you must work harder to win acceptance, you are willing to take insults and disrespect to make the relationship work.

5. Since you do not see the unhealthiness of the relationship, you are blinded to the disrespect and insults of others.

Your self-confidence is very low, and you struggle to emotionally and physically stand up for yourself.

When you do not feel good about yourself and struggle to express your feelings, you believe it is almost impossible to stand up to a distrustful and disrespectful mate. You do not have much trust in relationships and chances are you do not have enough confidence in yourself to change your situation. If you live with a mate that controls with anger or verbal threats, you feel even more powerless in the already helpless situation. Regardless of how you are being treated, you need to always remember that God created you with feelings and you should be allowed to express those feelings. The longer you hold your feelings inside, the more those suppressed feelings will weigh you down and make you feel helpless in your situation. This will be discussed in more detail later in the book.

Since your mate has not been able to fulfill your emotional needs, you blame him or her for not living up to their part of the relationship, believing you can't make a difference in the relationship until your mate changes.

If you did not receive much love and attention from your caregivers as a child, you would naturally have a strong desire to fill those emotional needs from someone as an adult. However, when you look to the adult relationship to fill the emotional needs, you become disappointed again when your mate does not fulfill those needs. The real problem typically is not that your mate does not love you; the core issue is that you chose a mate that does not know how to love you (similar to your caregivers). Secondly, even if your mate did suddenly change by showing you love and attention, you would most likely not know how to accept that love since you are not accustomed to receiving it. Regardless of the reason for not receiving love, it is easier to point the finger at your mate believing nothing can happen unless he or she changes. You will never be emotionally fulfilled if you look to your mate for the love you did not receive as a child. The reason for this is that you cannot fill an emotional emptiness created in childhood through the love of an adult relationship. You must resolve your past emptiness before you can fully accept the love from another adult. Both partners need to learn how to give and receive love.

You tend to live more with the dream of what an emotionally close relationship could be than with the reality of your situation.

After many years of trying to make the relationship work, you will be unable to see the reality of how unhealthy your situation truly has become. You do not see how much you are allowing your unemotional partner to remain unhealthy when you do everything to make the relationship work. When you are consumed with making things work you neglect your own needs, wants, and desires with the hope that someday you will have a loving relationship. Unfortunately, that "someday" never comes and you find yourself dried up emotionally to the point of dying inside before you get help for yourself. If you are working harder and taking on more responsibility than your partner (and your partner has the capability to do more), something is definitely wrong. Your mate is taking advantage of you. Marriage is supposed to be helping each other continually work toward the goal of developing a mutually loving, helpful, and respectful relationship. That is why you are called "helpmates."

WORDS OF ENCOURAGEMENT

Realizing you are living in an emotionless relationship ironically brings a host of emotions whirling around like an irritating sandstorm or blistering tornado. Over time, your frustration can build to anger, especially after you exhaust all the different ways you try to change your mate into the warm emotional person you thought you married. Take heart. As you read you will learn more that you can do to make a difference in your relationship. Remember, God "gives strength to the weary and increases the power of the weak," (Isaiah 40:29).

Personal Reflection

May I accept help to open my eyes
to the love that is sent my way and open my heart to accepting that love.

≈

STUDY QUESTIONS

1. How have your past relationships affected your ability to have a trusting, close relationship with your mate, even with God?

2. Describe how you will work harder, wait longer, and do whatever it takes in order to receive love and attention from your mate.

3. Describe how you become uncomfortable when you receive affection?

4. Describe how you put others before yourself to the point of excluding your own feelings and needs.

5. Describe how you are willing to endure more insults and less respect.

6. Describe how you struggle to emotionally and physically stand up for yourself.

7. Describe how you blame your mate for not living up to their part of the relationship.

8. Describe how you are more aware of your dream to have an emotionally close relationship than the reality of your situation.

9. After reading this chapter, what additional insights have you learned about yourself and what can you do to change your life for the better?

6

WOMEN WANT A RELATIONSHIP, MEN WANT SEX!

Men want to be right; women need to be heard.

Jerry and Ruth had an argument two days ago and Jerry knew he messed up. As usual, he had a hard time expressing his feelings, especially the words "I'm sorry," which was not in his vocabulary anyway. Instead of words, Jerry performed his usual ritual of making up through the act of buying forgiveness. This time, he tried to mend the situation with flowers.

Without saying anything, Jerry handed over a big colorful bouquet with a sheepish grin on his face. Ruth looked at the flowers, forcing out a halfhearted "thanks." Even though Ruth loves flowers, Jerry's gifts always seem too little, too late. Accepting gifts, instead of his words of forgiveness, bring an ache to her heart, making her feel she is not good enough for his love or settling for second best. Ruth feels cheated by his gifts and has become numb to the lack of emotion in the relationship. She always dreamed of a loving marriage, but she never expected her marriage to turn into such a disappointment. Ruth has become resigned to living this way, since she doesn't know what else to do.

Jerry can sense that all too familiar cold attitude coming from Ruth like a bucket of cold water in his face. Ruth's silence and refusal to make dinner for three days is the "two by four" across Jerry's thick head that helps him see she is upset with him. This only makes him become more uncomfortable inside with pangs of guilt. Later that night, Jerry dances around Ruth with his usual "let's-have-sex-to-make-things-better" ritual. Tired of the turmoil in the relationship, Ruth again surrenders her body for the sake of survival, believing it is the Christian thing to do. Besides, she realized early in the relationship, she must surrender to keep peace. After having sex, Jerry leaves the bedroom to move on to other things, believing any problems have been solved and lifted off his shoulders. Ruth remains limp in bed with that familiar empty feeling resonating through her body. Somehow, she tries to be grateful for the brief time spent together, while denying her feelings. She musters up the motivation to shake off the hurt in order to, once again, let it go. However, this time, Ruth has trouble letting go of the hurt and disappointment so she stuffs the pain inside.

INTERPRETING SEX DIFFERENTLY

Relationships like Jerry and Ruth's are very common where the unemotional man is clueless to understanding the meaning of becoming sexually close or "intimate" with his wife. Similarly, women do not understand what sex means for the unemotional man. In the book, *Why Men Don't Listen and Women Can't Read Maps,* the authors, Barbara and Allan Pease, summarize some of the differences this way: "A man needs to be trained in the art of pleasuring a woman—it does not come naturally to him. He's a hunter—he's wired to solve problems, chase lunch, and fight enemies. At the end of the day, he just wants to fire gaze and give a few pelvic thrusts to keep his tribe populated. For a woman to feel the desire for sex, she needs to feel loved, adored, and significant. Now here's the twist that most people never realize: A man needs to have sex before he can get in tune with his feelings. Unfortunately, a woman needs him to do that first before she's turned on to sex."[9] Sadly, the difference in how men and women think and act about intimacy is rarely revealed until after much damage has occurred far into the relationship. Those couples that have learned from talking about their differences or seek counsel to work out their issues are much more likely to succeed.

SEX AND THE UNEMOTIONAL MATE

Since emotions are not part of the equation of the relationship, the unemotional mate is blind to the emotional needs of the partner. The emotional emptiness does not allow the person to detect true emotion or have the sensory capacity to emotionally connect—creating emptiness in the relationship. In addition, the unemotional mate has a selfish drive to satisfy sexual needs and fill his own personal emotional emptiness. This is where sex enters into the equation. Not only can sex be a physical release, it also provides a heightened physical satisfaction that is the closest the unemotional mate can experience with an emotion. The sexual experience becomes the closest to "feeling love," or "becoming close." Consequently, the feeling of being close or feeling loved is often equated with the act of sex, increasing the importance of the time, amount, and occasion of sex. The more insecure and/or unloved the unemotional mate feels, the more he or she will expect (or demand) the sexual needs to be met. Having sex is also used as a means to relieve tension or create a sense of security to bring everything back to a state of normalcy. This is especially true after some conflict. Sex is believed to be the means to vanquish all wrongdoings, since words are not adequate to settle or calm the issue. If the emotional mate (mostly women) responds with sex as a way to comply, give in, or help bring peace to an issue, that response sends the message that the unemotional mate is forgiven, free from guilt, or can go back to the old ways. Giving sex to the unemotional mate after a conflict only encourages the unemotional partner to use sex as a pacifier for problems and disregards the need to talk out the issues.

SEX AND THE EMOTIONAL MATE

How the unemotional mate interprets sex is extremely confusing, frustrating, and disappointing for the emotional partner. This is especially true for women who interpret intimacy as a sacred form of being connected with the man she considers the most important person in her life. She envisions spending that intimate time together as a testimony of the sacred bond she desires to create with the man of her dreams. When the man of her dreams treats that intimate time simply as a selfish physical act for satisfying his own needs, it's worse than devastating. It adds up to a meaningless act that turns women away in disgust. When the unemotional man acts as if he totally disregards that sacred time, the woman feels deceived, emotionally abandoned, and used like a prostitute. Instead, women want to be romantic, appreciated, talked with, held, kissed, which all add up to being loved. Lovemaking is an intimate, passionate time of showing how much you mean to the other person. Unless the couple can climb past their selfish desires, sexual intimacy will be doomed to being a meaningless act.

IMPROVING INTIMACY

When sex is great for both partners, the whole relationship improves because you both are getting what you want. Women desire to be tenderly touched and held with a caring conversation about the relationship before and during the sexual experience. However, men are not typically verbal, especially during sex. If the man stops talking, the woman may think he isn't interested. The man is very interested in the experience, he just has a hard time enjoying the moment and becoming verbally expressive at the same time. Sometimes men (especially insecure men) become distracted when the women talks, which may hinder his sexual response. The reason for this comes from his inability to verbally respond and perform to the expectations of his mate. Usually the man puts these expectations on himself. Often, this situation is helped when the man improves his confidence through counseling.

Men: When you meet your wife's needs sexually, you will receive more in return. To show you are interested in your mate, ask her what she needs, learn to be more romantic, use tender touch, and just talk with her to increase the fulfillment of your wife's sexual needs.

Women: When you meet your husband's needs sexually, you will receive more in return. At the same time, you need to learn to talk less during sex and use vocal sounds to show you're enjoying (hopefully you are) the experience in order to fulfill the man's sexual needs. Women, do not assume your mate knows how to touch you or talk to you the way you want. Even if you have been married for years most men are too embarrassed to admit they do not know how to make love to their wife so they just muddle through, only to destroy the experience. If you desire to be loved, do not let your personal issues (anger or resentment) get in the way of teaching your mate how to be intimate

DON'T STOP TRYING TO BE INTIMATE

1. "Husbands, love your wives, just as Christ loved the church and gave himself up for her to make her holy, cleansing her by the washing with water through the word, and to present her to himself as a radiant church, without stain or

wrinkle or any other blemish, but holy and blameless. In this way, husbands ought to love their wives as their own bodies. He who loves his wife loves himself," (Ephesians 5:25–28). This is good advice. Men, if you do not know how to have an intimate relationship with your wife, don't despair; you're in good company with most men. However, don't rest until you learn how to become intimate. I strongly recommend you do the following:

- Ask your wife how you can love her. Don't be embarrassed, just ask her. After you pick her up from fainting, she would be glad to tell you (unless she is not talking to you right now). Write down what she tells you. Don't be afraid to ask her for more clarification if you do not understand *how* she wants you to do something.

- Daily pray this prayer: *God, I give you my life to mold me into the loving husband You want me to be. Forgive my spirit of insensitivity, selfishness, pride, and hardened heart. My Father in Heaven, fill me with Your Spirit of sensitivity, selflessness, loving kindness, with an emotional heart. I claim these things in Jesus Christ's name.*

- Everyday for one week, read 2 Corinthians 13 (the Love Chapter). Before you read, ask God to help you understand His Word and His direction to put it into practice.

- Go to the bookstore to find practical material for creating a relationship.

- Find a mature person to talk with (friend, pastor, or counselor) to learn about how to develop a better relationship by loving your wife.

2. "The husband should fulfill his marital duty to his wife, and likewise the wife to her husband," (1 Corinthians 7:3). Women, if your husband has difficulty showing you love,

do not assume he knows how to love you. Just because he is married to you doesn't mean he knows how to love you. I recommend you do the following:

- Talk to your man and teach him how to love you! If you have anger toward your husband for not loving you, you are responsible for creating a greater wedge between you.

- Daily pray this prayer: *God, I give you my life to mold me into the loving wife that You want me to be. Forgive my spirit of insensitivity and hardened heart toward my husband. My Father in Heaven, fill me with Your Spirit of sensitivity, lovingkindness, and an emotional heart. I claim these things in Jesus Christ's name.*

- Every day for one week, read 2 Corinthians 13 (the Love Chapter). Before you read, ask God to help you understand His Word and His direction to put it into practice.

- Go to the bookstore to find practical material for creating a relationship.

- Find a mature person to talk with (friend, pastor, or counselor) to learn about how to develop a better relationship by loving your husband.

Personal Reflection
May I accept help to see my mate through new eyes, to hear my mate through new ears, and to be sensitive to my mate through a new heart.

≈

STUDY QUESTIONS

1. Describe how your definition of sexual intimacy differs from your mate's definition.

2. How do the differences make you feel and affect your relationship?

3. How have the physical/sexual desires changed over the course of the relationship?

4. Describe what the scripture Ephesians 5:25–28 means to you.

5. Describe what the scripture 1 Corinthians 7:3 means to you.

6. After reading this chapter, what additional insights have you learned about yourself and what can you do to change your life and relationship for the better?

7

UNDERSTANDING THE EMOTIONAL DIFFERENCES

Your differences are what should bring you together, not split you apart.

You may wonder how you became so different from your mate. To help answer this question, let's start at the beginning. Interestingly, God created all embryos to begin life "female" in nature with the fetus starting out very similar in all areas of the brain and body. The brain was created with two sides that have separate functions that work together. The left side is analytical, examines cause and effect, breaks things down into facts, objectives, and relates through talking[10] (good for following directions, listening, using symbols, talking and reciting). Where as the right side of the brain uses imagination, intuition, forms images and mental combinations, is subjective, and relates through relationships[11] (good for art, music, sports, and building relationships). A massive intertwining of nerve fibers allows both sides to function beautifully together. Approximately the seventh week of pregnancy a strong dose of the hormone, testosterone, covers the male fetus to masculinize the body. At that point, something startling happens to the male fetus. This hormonal covering actually damages the brain and alters how it functions. (Men, this information is dangerous if left in the wrong hands!) The nerve fibers that connect the two sides of the brain become damaged, making the flow of information from one side to the other, less efficient.[12]

BLAME IT ON TESTOSTERONE

Testosterone can be blamed for men thinking longer about what he believes and the delay in a response when there is some emotional content to the issue. Men still have the ability to think and feel, however, it takes longer for the message to transfer from one side of the brain to the other. (Men, this information could wipe out our "excuse" strategy.) In comparison, a woman maintains the original brain functioning and is able to more effectively utilize both sides of the brain and respond more quickly to feelings and information with feeling content.

Now ladies, don't go telling everyone you finally found the secret why your husband is the way he is; there is more to the story. Testosterone may give some answers for the difference in responding, but you probably would say, "When he wants something (like sex), he doesn't have a problem responding quickly." (Actually, he may respond too quickly.) Although hormone change is a core reason why men and women relate differently to the world, the difference should not be used as an excuse for men to remain unemotional. There are many more reasons for the personality differences, which will be discussed throughout the book.

LOGIC FIRST, FEELINGS SECOND

Jennifer recalled how crushed she felt when a neighbor made an unkind comment about a recipe she had shared with her a week earlier. For several days, Jennifer was quiet and could not say anything nice about her neighbor. Jennifer's husband, Brad, could not understand the problem. "It's only a recipe; get over it," he would say. Of course, Brad's comments only stabbed Jennifer in the heart even more.

"Not only does my neighbor say nasty things, my husband doesn't care about what I say either," Jennifer said with tears in her eyes. She has always regretted telling Brad her feelings, knowing it would end up back in her face or become part of some joke later on.

The unemotional person (often the man) may make the comment to Jennifer, "It's only a recipe; get over it" or "What is all the big fuss all about—you're being sooo emotional!" The unemotional man has little space in his life for all the "whining" that does not make sense to him. Whether unemotional or not, men are wired to first understand how and why something happens before emotion becomes a part of the response. An unemotional man's brain organizes, evaluates, and has more of a relationship with objects than humans. Unemotional men feel more in control with objects and especially enjoy that objects don't talk back! Men must sort out the pieces by logically taking the situation apart, working it out, and putting it back together before he can understand the situation in his own way. The man uses a "fix-it" approach to just about everything as a way to move on with life. This is mostly due to the man's logical mind needing to rationally understand how he fits in with situations and his natural ability to compartmentalize life. Once the man understands the issues, then and only then, can he move on to the emotional side of the issue.

For the unemotional person, emotions only get in the way of thinking rationally and making decisions. Having emotions creates a sense of being out of control for the logical person. Emotions represent vulnerability, weakness, and sometimes the fear that something bad may happen. The woman needs to help the man work through the situation by letting him dissect it, logically understand it, and fix it in his own mind. Then he will be better able to move closer to the emotional part.

FEELING FIRST, LOGIC SECOND

The emotionally minded person (often the woman) would comment to the rational man, "Why are you making such a fuss over that new truck? Why don't you make a fuss over me?" Women don't understand why a man has more emotion about the *things* in life than with people. This sends confusing messages, only building disappointment when the emotional mate does not get the love he or she expects. Similar to Jennifer's reaction to her husband Brad, I often hear women with heartbreaking stories about their insensitive partner giving a deaf ear, insults, or joking remarks, after the woman expresses feelings. It becomes disappointing and hurtful to the emotional mate when feelings are not as important or accepted compared to other areas of the partner's life. This scenario happens more in the emotionless relationship than people are willing to admit, believing they are destined to live that way.

Women deal with life first by relating emotionally and socially. This is why Jennifer's heart was crushed when the neighbor made an unkind comment about the recipe she had shared a week earlier. Jennifer's sharing of the recipe was a form of connecting, reaching out, and sharing part of her. However, if the recipe was rejected, Jennifer felt rejected. This is one of the biggest differences between men and women. The man interprets giving the recipe not as a relationship but simply as the giving of information. Jennifer interpreted the information as sharing part of her life. Once a woman talks or cries out what she feels, she becomes more logical. The man needs to help the woman work through the situation by letting her cry and talk out how she feels about the situation. Then she will be able to move closer to the logical part.

EXPRESSING ANGER

Ironically, even when men (or women) are considered unemotional, they still have the capacity to express large amounts of emotion, particularly anger. Often anger can accumulate and become explosive when something doesn't go his way or when he feels powerless. For example, when you have been a victim of hurt in the past and you felt powerless to do anything about it, those same feelings can come up again when you feel like a victim as an adult. Anger is a way to shield you from hurt and gives a sense of power, especially when something was unjustly done to you. Power is the ability to get what you want; anger is the means to exercise power when faced with the loss or threat of losing what you have.[13] When the unemotional person does not get his way, anger often comes out stronger since the new situation triggers the old suppressed feelings of helplessness. Consequently, the person will feel justified in his anger as a way to never let anyone put them in a position of being helpless or powerless again.

Living with a person that exhibits emotional outbursts can be very scary and confusing, especially when you never know when the anger will strike. When you are desperate for the relationship to work, you will put up with years of verbal outbursts and negative emotion that can make you feel emotionally numb. You shut off your feelings in order to survive. Although most family members learn over time what triggers the person into anger, you live with a constant apprehension that something could happen anytime. You walk on eggshells and don't realize that you are being victimized by how you are being treated. Whether you are the angry partner or you are living with an angry mate, I strongly recommend both of you get counseling for your situation. Anger that is hurtful, threatening, disrespectful, and full of rage, is inappropriate and should not be accepted or tolerated in any home. It is very harmful to everyone, especially to the heart and mind of children.

If you are living with an angry mate, I recommend you:

1. Begin praying for physical and emotional strength, for the right words and actions towards the other person;.

2. In a calm voice, verbalize what you do not like about what he or she does and that you want it to stop.

3. If you are afraid or unable to change the situation with words, remove yourself from the situation when he or she gets angry.

4. Get counseling to help you remain strong and learn how to handle the difficult situations.

THE DIFFERENCES CAN COMPLEMENT EACH OTHER

God actually knew what He was doing when he created man and woman to function very differently. The saying "opposites attract" is truer than you may give credit. Women were created with a greater ability to perceive what is happening around them (intuition) and the ability to accurately identify needs, desires, wants, and displeasures in order to increase control over the stresses of life. Men were created with a greater ability to be effectively practical and develop a sense of trust to build security and safety with those around them. Men tend to have a greater ability to logically relate with people and things, providing a great strength to initiate rational thinking to accurately understand the reasons why situations happen.

You need those opposites to function more effectively and efficiently together. For example, when there is a decision to be made, the emotional attributes of one partner and the logical attributes of the other should work together for a more balanced decision. You do not want to make a decision solely based on emotions and later regret the decision. For the same reason, you do not want to make a decision based solely on logic without considering the personal effects of that decision. The attributes of each partner should complement each other, creating a well-functioning union.

WORDS OF ENCOURAGEMENT

If you have not healed the original wounds from past relationships, those wounds can become the "baggage" you will carry into your future relationships. When you take the original differences between men and women and combine your unhealthy baggage, you are certain to have relationship problems. The more unhealthy baggage you have in your own life, the more insecure you will be. The more insecure you are, the more defensive you will become with others. The more defensive you become the less likely you will get along with your mate. Marital difficulties are created from one partner triggering the other partner's baggage. When each partner heals his or her own personal baggage, the relationship will ultimately become healthier. Take responsibility of your own baggage rather than trying to change those of your mate.

Personal Reflection

May I learn to appreciate the differences in my mate,
especially when I don't understand those differences.
And may I find the strength and patience to learn.

≈

STUDY QUESTIONS

1. Who is more logical and who is more emotional in your relationship?

2. Describe how the differences between you and your mate affect your relationship.

3. Is there someone you know that has outbursts of emotion? If so, how does it affect you and your relationship?

4. How can your emotional differences complement your relationship?

5. After reading this chapter, what additional insights have you learned about yourself and what can you do to change your life and your relationship for the better?

8

DANCING THE
RELATIONSHIP TANGO
(Struggling with becoming emotionally close)

~

*The person doing the most blaming is usually
the person who is the most to blame.*

Joe was looking at me shaking his head in bewilderment about his difficulty in feeling close with his wife Marcy. He said, "Whenever my relationship appears to be going well with Marcy, something always seems to happen. I just don't understand it." Joe continued showing frustration in his face, "If we go out together and have a good time, on the way home we start arguing about stupid little things that don't make sense." I asked Joe how often and how long this pattern was going on between them. He looked up at the ceiling as if he was looking for the answers. After a moment, he straightened his head and looked at me with amazement, "I never thought of it before, but as long as I can remember it almost seems like every time things seem to go well, something happens to ruin how we get along." I have called the problems with Joe and Marcy, The Relationship Tango. It is one of the most common forms of relationship dysfunction that devastates the heart and cripples the relationship bond. It is usually difficult to see this problem within your relationship, unless someone points it out.

CYCLE OF PULL-PUSH

Here is how the Relationship Tango happens. You begin doing some activity with your mate such as going out for dinner or watching a movie. You may start to feel some closeness or have some common bond which makes you feel good. After a period of time, for little reason, something happens that irritates you. Someone says something you don't like or does something that sets someone off. Harsh words are exchanged, there's a disagreement and someone blows up. You argue and eventually go your separate ways in frustration or anger.

The origin of this cycle usually stems from your past hurtful, disappointing circumstances or relationships that broke your heart. For example, with little warning your parents separated and eventually divorced when you were eight years old. That family unity in your home was destroyed and you felt a great loss. Whether your experiences in life included divorce, separation, illness, death, neglect, or abuse with the ones you loved, those hurts left a lasting, painful impression. When your heart is broken you become afraid to get too close to people for fear of becoming emotionally hurt again. Typically, the hurts are held so deeply inside you are not aware of the fear. Each time your heart is broken with someone you have a close connection with the harder it will be for you to connect with the next important relationship. All you know is that you don't want to be hurt again so you keep your distance to protect your heart.

It is natural for you to want attention and love from your mate so you will try to pull him or her toward you to get that love. However, if your past hurts have not been healed, you will continue to be afraid to get too close. The problem is you cannot see this cycle happening because you have lived this way with most (or all) your relationships. When you start feeling close, an incident stirs up the old fear and you want to push that feeling away. As a result, you push away the person and love you desire to have.

CYCLE OF PULL-PUSH

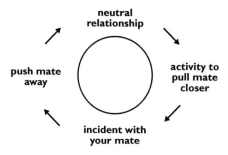

Chances are you have been reacting to this cycle for so long you cannot see how it affects your relationship. When you have difficulty getting emotionally close, you will more often become upset or disappointed toward your mate. You will be the one doing more of the blaming and accusing because you do not see these traits within yourself. The source of the relationship disagreements is often the very person creating the arguments. This cycle creates extreme confusion, heartache, frustration, and hurt within the relationship, which consequently causes resentment toward each other. If this cycle is not changed it can lead to emotional and physical distancing and eventual devastation of the relationship. The following characteristics may determine if you are dancing the Relationship Tango:

You grew up in a home where your emotional needs were not met, and you have a hard time feeling emotionally close in adult relationships

Marcy grew up in a home where her parents worked many hours, leaving little time for the family relationships. She described fond memories of her father when he was around, but admitted to being disappointed since he was frequently gone. After high school, she had dreams of marrying the boy she dated for three years. One day, unexpectedly, the boy left her for another girl. In counseling, Marcy realized she had been hurt by the important people in her past, and she found herself in a relationship similar to the type of relationship she had with her parents.

The past hurtful relationships create the belief that getting emotionally close to someone may be too risky. For example, in Marcy's desperate attempt to fill the childhood emptiness created by the lack of love and attention, Marcy was more accustomed to relationships where the man was emotionally unavailable. As a result, Marcy had a very hard time allowing herself to receive love and attention again as an adult.

After a period of time of becoming close with your mate, you feel uncomfortable and push your mate away

Marcy realized she craved activities to get love and attention from her mate but something always happened to ruin the activity. "It was so strange," she once commented, "when we do something together we can have a good time. But as my husband spends too much time with me, I start to get uncomfortable. It never fails, we have an argument and the time is ruined."

If you are receiving love and affection, old fears may become stirred inside which make you, "uncomfortable," "smothered," "closed in," "trapped," or "need space" when you are too close. These feelings cause you to irrationally react to something the other person said or did. Oftentimes the disagreements are over small issues that get blown out of proportion. This way of living traps you into the miserable position of desperately wanting to be loved by someone, but pushing away the love you receive because you don't know how to receive it.

You are accustomed to pursuing love and affection from someone emotionally unavailable

Marcy remembered how her heart ached as she dreamed of doing things with her father, only to be disappointed when he did not have time for her. Since her father was also emotionally unavailable, Marcy continually pursued her father to receive the love and affection she desired. As a result of Marcy's repeatedly unsuccessful attempts to receive his love, she grew up becoming more accustomed to pursuing love from men that were emotionally and physically distant or unavailable.

You have frequent arguments or misunderstandings that spoil your good time together

The dilemma that Joe and Marcy had is very typical of the Relationship Tango. In your desire to have a good time, something usually happens to spoil the time together. As Joe commented, "Whenever my relationship appears to be going well with Marcy, something always seems to happen. I just don't understand it. If we go out together and have a good time, on the way home we start arguing about stupid little things that don't make sense." The wounded partner that has the most difficulty getting close will usually blame something on the other person or allow some other circumstance to interrupt your plans. The more afraid a partner is to get close, the more often arguments will be started to keep the distance. Just like in the scenario with Joe, the argument will catch you off guard and you will not understand why it is happening. Like Marcy, you will never admit the problem within yourself and you will always believe your mate is trying to hurt you. Unfortunately, your relationship becomes constantly challenged with issues between each other creating this never ending cycle of pull-push with the inability to feel close for long periods of time.

You have a hard time forgiving or giving in to the other person, frequently ending the day with unresolved issues

When you have been hurt in relationships, you will be more careful not to get hurt again. The more hurt you have received in the past, the more difficulty you will have forgiving or giving in to another person that may hurt you. Have you heard the old saying, 'Hurt me once, shame on you; hurt me twice, shame on me'? That saying represents how people naturally build up defenses to avoid being hurt again. The more hurt you have festering inside the less likely you will let your defenses down in order to forgive. Similarly, the more you believe you have been wronged, the less likely you will let go of issues and the less likely you will forgive.

There are minimal amounts of tender touching between you and your mate

If you are accustomed to loss of love (such as people leaving you) or minimal amounts of tender touches (hugs, kisses, etc.) from people in your life, you will typically not know how to give or accept love and tender touches in the future. Besides, if you are afraid of being emotionally close, having someone tenderly touch you is allowing someone to get too close. This can be very confusing for your partner when you constantly ask for quality time together and something always happens to get in the way of that time. Consequently, as much as you say you want your mate to touch you, you will become uncomfortable after you start receiving it. This can be very confusing and difficult to see in your own life. You are probably saying, "Why would I push attention away? That is what I don't get enough of!" The next time you receive tender touches, allow yourself to enjoy it. (You deserve it.)

STOP DANCING THE RELATIONSHIP TANGO

A bit of warning: If you recognize these characteristics in

your relationship do not immediately accuse your mate of possessing these characteristics. The more you try to point to your mate as being the problem, the more you will be considered the enemy. I recommend you follow Matthew 7:5 as your guide. "You hypocrite, first take the plank out of your own eye, and then you will see clearly to remove the speck from your brother's eye." Look at what you need to change in your own life to be an example for your mate (and children). Whether you see these characteristics in your mate or within yourself, you must identify and heal your own issues before you can help someone else. The following are steps to begin a process of healing:

1. **Pray about your situation. See chapter "Finding Strength Through Prayer"**

2. **Both partners should seek counseling to:**
    - Identify your own past hurts
    - Find healing to your own issues
    - Identify how your mate triggers your unhealthy past and present issues
    - Learn where in the past your issues are from; e l i m i-nate those past issues
    - Learn what to do with your attitudes and behaviors that are triggered
    - Learn how to communicate your feelings and learn how to listen to your mate's feelings
    - Learn how to show and receive both love and respect
    - Learn how to survive with an unemotional mate
    - See appendix for information regarding "How to find a counselor"

3. **Change how you respond to your mate**
    One of the hardest things for a mate is to hold your tongue

and remain calm when your partner says something nasty or does something hurtful. Try not to become defensive or over-react when your mate accuses you of something and wants to stop or change the activity with you. Whatever accusation you throw back, will be used against you to start World War III. The wounded mate will use whatever possible to push you away. You will never win with an irrationally thinking, emotionally defensive mate. His or her woundedness will be triggered even more with any insults you throw back. Don't play the game. If you see your mate getting upset, begin to pray inside to stop your tongue from firing back and separate your emotions from your mate's. Don't stoop to that immature level and argue back. You are worth more than that, and it is not worth your effort.

4. **Make observations how you and your mate respond to each other**

The more you identify the cycle of Relationship Tango in your relationship, the more you will have a better under-standing of why you react the way you do toward each other. Hopefully, your increased understanding will reduce your own negative reactions and improve your response.

5. **Make calm, peaceful comments about what you observe**

If you want to make an observation to your mate about his or her reaction, do not bring up your comments during the heat of an argument or when either one of you is emotionally upset. When the situation has cooled down and your mate is able to talk more rationally, make comments to your mate. Start with a positive comment about the issue or a compliment to begin on a positive note. If you immediately start a conversation with a negative comment about the other person, the walls of defen-siveness will go up automatically. As a result, your mate will not be listening to anything else you say.

For example, if you and your mate frequently have arguments after you have a nice night out, you may say, "Marcy, I did have a nice night out. I'm glad we went. You know, I was thinking, it seems interesting that we have arguments after we have a good time. Have you ever noticed that?" The comment started with a compliment, keeping the focus on "we" or "I," not using the accusatory "you" statement. If you're speaking to a man and he does not respond right away, give him some time to think about it. Come back to it later. Men typically are thinkers and take longer to respond to a question about emotions.

6. Do not stop trying to love your partner

Trying to love a person who has been emotionally wounded throughout their past is like trying to fill a bottomless pit with water from a garden hose. You cannot fill the original emotional emptiness created in childhood with love from an adult relationship. That is why you can continually show love to a person but it never seems to satisfy their needs or seems to be good enough. You can be the nicest person and always do more for your mate, but they never seem to appreciate what you do. Your mate may have a bottomless pit of needing attention or needing things done for them. However, this pit was created in childhood when the primary caregivers did not give that original love and attention. That pit must be filled by finding healing from whatever created the hurt. For example, if your father died or was not there physically, the hurt from that loss must be healed through counseling and/or faith in God to fill that emptiness. If your partner pushes you away when you give love, he or she will continue to push you away until the old wounds are identified and healed.

7. Find time for yourself

Whatever happens between you and your mate, do not

stop taking good care of yourself. Find time to pray, talk to a trusted friend, seek counseling, and write your thoughts in a journal. Find enjoyable activities such as a hobby, reading, bike riding, etc., that you can do on a regular basis to take your mind off the problems of your relationship. Most specifically, pray for guidance, strength, and the perseverance to continue loving your partner. Begin to allow yourself to separate your emotions from those of your partner. In other words, recognize your partner has difficulty relating to you and do not allow yourself to become pulled into an argument over some small problem that he or she uses as an excuse not to get close.

8. If you are the person afraid to get close and notice these characteristics in yourself, tell your mate ahead of time that you want to change how you respond and follow the steps listed below.

- When you begin to feel uncomfortable, smothered, etc., notice those feelings and remind yourself of your desire to be close.
- Begin talking or writing out your feelings.
- Give yourself permission to accept the affection from your mate.
- Ask your mate to be patient with you and have your mate ask how you feel when the situation becomes uncomfortable.
- Pray to become more accepting of affection given to you.
- Seek counseling to overcome this cycle.

WORDS OF ENCOURAGEMENT

If you have difficulty getting close to people, do not despair.

The reason for this chapter is to let you know how common this struggle is in relationships. God wants you to have a loving, joyful relationship with your mate. Pray for the insight to understand the reasons why you respond this way. "Two are better than one, because they have a good return for their work: If one falls down, his friend can help him up. But pity the man who falls and no one to help him up!" (Ecclesiastes 4:9–10)

Personal Reflection
Allow my heart to be open when I receive love,
protect my heart when I receive hurt,
and help me to learn to know the difference.

STUDY QUESTIONS

1. Describe any cycle of pull-push emotional closeness you see within yourself or your partner that may determine you are dancing the Relationship Tango.

2. Describe any past negative experience with a relationship that may have contributed to this cycle of behavior.

3. How does the scripture, Matthew 7:5, apply to your life?

4. What can you do to help change the Relationship Tango that occurs in your life?

5. After reading this chapter, what additional insights have you learned about yourself and what can you do to change your life and your relationship for the better?

9

SHOWING INTEREST IN EVERYTHING ELSE BUT YOU

~

*"For where your treasure is, there your
heart will be also," (Matthew 6:21)*

Peter came to my office because his wife, Tammy, was
threatening to leave him. Peter thought the relationship was
going "Okay," even though he worked sixty hours per week and
went out with the guys a couple of nights each week. Because he
worked long hours, he didn't see any problem with the time he
spent away from home to unwind. "Besides," Peter explained to
justify himself, "whenever I tried to help at home it was never
good enough for Tammy." Peter complained that Tammy was
involved in too many activities away from home that unfairly
put more of the home responsibilities on him.

When I met with Tammy, her interpretation was worlds
apart from Peter's. Tammy said they were so much in love
during the courtship, but she had become heartbroken as their
relationship became distant over the years. The time Peter was
away from home left little quality time with her or the children. With some anger in her voice, Tammy didn't hesitate to
mention the weekends Peter was away for sporting tourna-
ments and being with the guys. Tammy described their relationship as nonexistent with rarely any signs of affection from
Peter—unless he wanted sex.

Peter's feeble attempts at helping with the kids made

Tammy's temper flare that much more. The reason why Tammy felt Peter was never good enough with the kids was because he was not around enough to know what to do. Tammy admitted to becoming more involved with activities outside the home as a way to feel good about herself and decrease the loneliness she experienced in the marriage. Peter's unsupportive comments regarding Tammy's interests only increased her resentment and furthered her belief that he did not care.

PURSUING INTERESTS OUTSIDE THE MARRIAGE

Unfortunately, it is very common for a mate like Peter to pursue more interests outside the marriage than maintain a relationship in the marriage. It is extremely common for the courtship to be like visiting Disneyland and the marriage to turn out like the long drive home. Before marriage, the couple is full of dreams (more from the woman) and promises (more from the man) in a relationship blinded by the belief that LOVE can cure anything and will forever shield your state of bliss. As with Tammy, she expected the dreams and promises to come true in a blissful relationship and Peter expected to continue his outside interests with his friends. Men like Peter often rationalize, "Since I've worked hard all day and need the relaxation, my wife should understand."

Like Peter, the unemotional mate would go on with life as if he is living in another world. He would seek his own selfish interests with little emotional investment in the family. This begins the loneliness of an emotionless relationship, leaving the spouse feeling abandoned, craving affection and attention. Often the emotional partner will carry into the marriage the hopes created during courtship, only to have those hopes shattered by the emotionally unavailable mate.

WHEN YOU ARE NOT EMOTIONALLY CONNECTED

The ironic thing is that, everyone, in some way, is seeking a connection to be loved, cared for, respected, and accepted. Typically, the emotional mate is the driving force with an emotional energy that tries to keep the relational fires burning. However, since the unemotional partner is incapable of emotionally relating, there is a desire to seek connections outside the relationship to satisfy his or her needs. The emotional mate becomes justifiably hurt by the partner's lack of emotional involvement, which gets worse as the unemotional mate continues to invest little into the marriage relationship. The following are characteristics of a person not able to show an interest in the mate:

You grew up in a home where you did not have emotionally close relationships

Your training ground for developing and maintaining relationships can be found during childhood years with the significant people in your life (parents, family, teachers, friends, etc). How they related to you and to each other is how you learned to have a relationship. If your parents did not have sit down conversations with you or show an interest in your activities, you are less likely to show an interest in the important people in your life. Even if you made a decision not to be like your parents, you would have little knowledge of what to do differently. Consequently, you would end up acting in many of the same ways as your parents. However, your past does not have to be your destiny. You have a choice to change how you are acting and relating to your family.

Your parent(s) did what they wanted, when they wanted

As much as Tammy complained about Peter being away from home, he could not understand why he had to stop seeing his friends or stop playing on his sport leagues. After all, Peter would contest, "I work long hours each week and deserve to have some fun." Peter never realized how much he was living like his father. Peter grew up in a home where his father worked long hours, six days a week and spent many nights out with his buddies playing sports or drinking beer. His mother often told Peter how much she hated his father being gone so much. However, his mother resigned herself to the lonely lifestyle, believing it was better for the children and better than living without a husband. Since his father could be away from the home and his mother allowed the behavior to continue, Peter believed Tammy should let him do the same.

A person can grow up mimicking the same unhealthy behaviors as a parent when the person admires the parent or when a child believes the best way to get close to an emotionally distant parent is to be just like the parent. As with Peter, many men that see their selfish fathers get away with whatever they want, whenever they want, will follow in their footsteps. Even if the wife voices her concerns, the man will often view those concerns similar to the nagging that his father received. The selfish behavior of one mate only serves to destroy the relationship.

You grew up in a home where you were able to either do what you wanted, when you wanted. Or, you were excessively restricted in what you could do.

Growing up Peter played outside for hours with his friends. At age sixteen he got a car, which opened the door to more freedom and even less time at home. His parents were busy people and did not put much restriction on Peter's activities. About a year after they were married, Tammy began to get irritated at how much time Peter spent with his buddies playing on sports leagues, fixing cars, and playing cards late into the night. Peter always became angry when Tammy tried to confine him to staying home.

As I mentioned previously, what happens in your childhood has a major influence in what you will do in adulthood. Peter never learned how to change the childhood lifestyle of doing what he wanted, when he wanted. That lifestyle continued into adulthood. At the same time, if you lived in a home opposite from Peter, where your caregivers were very strict, heavy with the rules and tough with punishment, chances are you will rebel in adulthood, wanting to do what you want, when you want, never again letting anyone tell you what to do.

You plan your life more around yourself rather than around other family members

Peter was not very emotionally close to his parents and he did not see emotions expressed by family members. He was expected to be responsible for many of his own personal needs since both his parents worked outside the home. Peter was proud he started working at age twelve in order to make his own spending money. Peter never realized that his unemotional and independent life as a child would make it difficult to relate to others later in life. Peter was so consumed with getting his own needs met in childhood that he never learned to think about anyone else. When you do not have the ability to relate with others, it is more common to think of your own needs above anyone else.

Your spouse tends to be the driving force for maintaining the relationship.

Out of her love for the family and desire to help Peter with his emotional limitations, Tammy does most of the talking during conversations and most of the planning for family activities. Often in emotionless relationships, one partner takes on the responsibility to make the relationship work while the other mate reaps the benefits. In her strong desire to make the relationship work or change Peter into the warm, loving helpmate she longed for, Tammy continues to make things work. As long as Tammy continues to take on the responsibility to do whatever it takes to make the relationship work, her actions are sending the message to Peter that he doesn't need to do anything to help the relationship. In essence, the harder Tammy works at maintaining the relationship, the less Peter has to put any effort into it. This message enables Peter to continue the irresponsible behaviors Tammy so desperately wants him to change.

FILLING THE EMPTINESS

If you are an unemotional person, you do not know what you are missing in a relationship, but you still have a need to fulfill your life with something meaningful. Your lifelong emptiness is what makes you seek interests outside the relationship to fulfill your own needs. The emptier you feel, the stronger the drive to fill that emptiness. Some of the more common pursuits are in the form of a hobby, sports activity, drinking, Internet surfing, sleeping, reading, computer games, spending money, television viewing, religion, working overtime, or just keeping busy. Since you are unable to fulfill the emptiness from relationships, the need to satisfy your emptiness is what lures you to find meaning in other areas of life. The need to fill the emptiness is what creates the craving for the activity. The more involved you are with the fulfillment activity, the stronger you believe the fulfillment is right for your life, regardless of how unhealthy the activities become.

WHEN YOUR PURSUITS ARE OUT OF CONTROL

The warning signs for when the pursuits are getting out

of control are when you become excessively consumed in other areas of your life to the exclusion and detriment of spending time in your relationship. The destructive pursuits that are used to fill your emptiness are activities such as affairs, hording, sexual perversion, pornography, gambling, alcohol, and drugs. If the person has been doing these activities long enough, they will always be able to find reasons to justify the need to continue. However, the only thing these activities will accomplish is a moral, emotional, mental, and spiritual decay of the individual and destruction of the family. These pursuits only lead to devastating consequences with a strong price to pay that is attached to each unhealthy behavior. The Bible addresses this in Galatians 5:19–21, "The acts of the sinful nature are obvious: sexual immorality, impurity and debauchery; idolatry and witchcraft; hatred, discord, jealousy, fits of rage, selfish ambition, dissensions, factions and envy; drunkenness, orgies, and the like. I warn you, as I did before, that those who live like this will not inherit the kingdom of God."

WHEN THE *EMOTIONAL MATE* SEEKS FULFILLMENT

Often, the lack of emotional involvement in a relationship will drive the emotional mate toward other activities to fill the emptiness felt inside. Filling the emptiness caused by an emotionless relationship will compel you to seek satisfaction in other areas of your life. The lack of emotion in the relationship eventually starves the emotional mate of the love they always longed for. As an emotional mate, when you do not feel loved and supported, you may retreat into activities to escape the feelings of anger, rejection, lack of love, and emotional abandonment. You may transfer your energy to activities with your children, church, work, hobbies, computer, television, reading, or other relationships. The unsupportive behavior of your spouse perpetuates the vicious cycle of rejection and faultfinding, which creates further emotional and physical separation and justifies each partner's activities outside the relationship.

When Peter returned home from work, everything would look as messy as when he left in the morning. "How come you haven't done anything except play on this computer," he bitterly complained to Tammy. She defended herself by pointing out how little he did to help her. Peter's frequent complaints seemed to be fruitless, only making Tammy ignore him even more. Tammy felt angry and hurt that Peter was not attentive to her emotional needs. The more Tammy tried to express how she felt, the more Peter would throw accusations about her poor housekeeping.

"Why should I care about anything, when I don't feel important?" Tammy said with anger. Since she thought her feelings were not important, she did not believe Peter cared about her. Feeling misunderstood and helpless to do anything about it, Tammy would sit at the computer to escape from the world of hurt and emptiness.

WHEN ACTIVITIES DIVIDE THE HEART

When you pursue interests outside the relationship, you become open to the danger of dividing your heart. Peter never realized how much his spending time with his buddies was irritating Tammy. Tammy never realized how much Peter was irritated by her lack of attention to him and the home. For all the time Peter spent outside the home giving attention to his friends and for the time Tammy was on the computer, they both were not giving love, attention, and respect to each other. The actions of Tammy and Peter spoke louder than words. The Bible is clear about the dangers of a divided heart. Matthew 6:21 reads, "For where your treasure is, there your heart will be also." No matter what interests grab your attention outside your relationship and family, those pursuits will eventually divide your time, energy, and devotion. You will eventually come face-to-face with decisions that will force you to make a choice that will no doubt become one of the toughest struggles in your life and tear your relationship apart, more than it already has been. For Tammy, it took being tired of living in misery to realize she needed to stop trying to change Peter to have a good marriage. For Peter, it took the desperate measures of Tammy threatening to leave for Peter's heart to be shattered in order for him to change. Peter's selfish choices made Tammy painfully aware of his misplaced priorities?

For a relationship to be focused in the right direction, your priorities need to include:

- First priority: Personal relationship with God (This refers to spending personal time with God and does not refer to putting religious activities first.)

- Second priority: Relationships with family (spouse first and children second)

- Third priority: Involvement with job

- Fourth priority: Time for yourself (if there is time)

The more activities that are before God and your mate, the more you will struggle in your relationship with God and your family.

PURSUING YOUR RELATIONSHIP

You may not like people telling you what to do, especially your mate. However, you must understand that your mate is NOT your enemy; the enemy is the dark forces in the world that want nothing more than to see you separated, divorced, and more miserable than you already are. When your mate tells you something, he or she is not nagging; but instead, trying to pursue or remind you the best way they know how. Your mate cannot change you directly; only you have control to change the course of fulfilling your needs and finding a satisfying relationship. If you spend more time with activities away from your family than you spend with your family, you have some serious thinking and praying to do. Your relationships should *not* be about you getting only *your* needs met. A relationship is about your *giving* to others. The saying "It's better to give than receive" is especially true for your time, energy, finances, and love to your family. You can gain more satisfaction and happiness from the satisfaction that you are giving to someone else. God has given you a relationship that will satisfy the emptiness in ways better than anything else you can pursue. However, you must make the choice to pursue your mate and family to make the relationship happen.

WORDS OF ENCOURAGEMENT

If you are the mate spending a lot of time in activities away from your family, you are showing where your heart is. Plain and simple, the time you choose to invest in your family will decide the dividends you will reap. If you are the mate spending a lot of time waiting for your partner to give you love, you may have a great amount of frustration, disappointment, and hurt. The longer you wait for your mate to fulfill your life, the longer you will be disappointed. As you learn to change how you live and respond to others, you will be less dependent on your mate and feel less helpless about your situation. Wherever you are, do not give up hope.

Personal Reflection
May the Lord be my strength and my shield;
when my heart trusts in him, I am helped.
(Psalms 28:7 Paraphrased)

≈

STUDY QUESTIONS

1. In what way is your relationship similar (or not similar) to Peter and Tammy's?

2. What characteristics of a person not showing an interest in a mate hits home for you?

3. What pursuits are interfering with your marriage and family relationships?

4. How can you alter your pursuits to improve your marriage and family relationships?

5. After reading this chapter, what additional insights have you learned about yourself and what can you do to change your life and your relationship for the better?

10

YOUR HEALTH AFFECTS
HOW YOU FEEL

~

How you take care of yourself can determine how you live.

Jerry came to see me because of the "pressure" from his wife. "If I don't change my involvement with the family, my wife threatened to kick me out," Jerry said with a tired look on his face. As I completed the mental health evaluation, Jerry mentioned he felt blah throughout the day and consequently didn't have much energy to do things with the family. He described his home life as demanding, as he tried to "please" his wife and kids. He did not sleep well and struggled to get up in the morning. He complained about being tired through the day (unless he had his quota of coffee or soda pop), as if all his energy was sapped out of him. By the time he got home from work, he felt like going to bed, which only added to his wife's list of complaints that he didn't do anything with the family. When I asked about his eating habits, he said breakfast was usually coffee, lunch was often fast foods, and he snacked on soda pop or junk food throughout the day. He did have a "meat and potato" dinner with a snack before bed (ice cream or cookies and milk). After hearing about Jerry's life, it was obvious his mind and body were exhausted, and he was suffering from depression. Similar to Jerry, unemotional people must get close to a disaster point before seeking help.

YOUR HEALTH IMPACTS HOW YOU FEEL

Your brain works like an electrical circuit box firing millions of impulses to activate your mind and body. As a high-functioning, living organism, your brain needs proper nutrients to fuel the circuits for proper firepower. Just reading the paper while munching on a donut and chugging a cup of coffee requires a great deal of brainpower. The food you put in your body has everything to do with how your body reacts. God created the brain to function at its best when fed by food that is alive with nutritional value, like vegetables, fruits, grains, or nuts. Many of the foods you eat may be processed, preserved, salted, sugared, and flavored, resulting in foods that are nutritionally dead.

With poor nourishment, your mind will think poorly, your senses will feel poorly, and your body will move poorly. It cannot be emphasized strongly enough how important the connection is between your physical body functioning and your emotional state of mind. Typically, people like Jerry who are emotionally stressed are more likely to have improper nutrition and unhealthy lifestyles that result in poor brain functioning. When you do not function well physically, you do not function well emotionally.

How you eat is vitally important to the way you feel and relate to others. The author and speaker Dr. Gary Smalley, devoted the book, *Love and Food,* to this subject. In his research, Dr. Smalley found there was a direct link between eating poorly and loving poorly, and a strong connection between healthy eating and healthy loving. People found their poor food choices led to indifference and withdrawal in their relationships. People who turned to processed foods for comfort often turn away from people they loved.[14] These people are temporarily feeling better in emotion and energy from the unhealthy foods they consume, instead of feeling good from the people or circumstances they are with. The following can be considered some of the worst and best foods for emotional health.

Worst for emotional health from high consumption of:

- White or refined sugar (soda pop, candy, sugar coated cereal, ice cream, etc.)

- White or refined flour (pasta, white rice, white bread, cake, etc.)

- Hydrogenated oils and animal fat (fried foods, chicken skins, vegetable oil, etc.)

- Chemically laden foods (preservatives, packaged meats, etc.)

Best for emotional health and brain functioning from consumption of:

- B vitamins, daily multiple vitamin, liquid minerals

- Raw honey and sweeteners from raw fruit (fructose)

- Whole-grain flour and whole grains (wholegrain breads, crackers, brown rice)

- Cold pressed oils and healthy fats (olive oil, flax seed oil, fish oils)

- Natural foods (raw fruits, vegetables, nuts)

Clearly, one of the biggest culprits that affects your mood is sugar. In the classic best seller, *Sugar Blues,* the author William Dufty points out that refined sugar is lethal when ingested by humans because it provides only what nutritionists describe as empty or naked calories. In addition, sugar is "worse than nothing" because it drains and leeches the body of precious vitamins and minerals through the demand its digestion, detoxification, and elimination make upon one's entire system.[15]

While the sugar is being absorbed into the blood, you feel a quick pickup. This surge of energy is succeeded by a sudden drop in blood sugar a few hours later. At that point, you are tired and feel emotionally blah, requiring more effort to move or even think until the blood sugar level is brought up again. Your brain functions poorly and you can be irritable, jumpy, and feeling lethargic. Anyone battling the "blahs" needs to realize the importance nutrition plays for proper emotion and brain functioning. Your body can actually crave sugar to fill the void left by the last sugar low. When you are at that low point chemically, you are also at a low point physically and emotionally.

According to Carolyn Dean, M.D., N.D., author of *Complementary Natural Prescriptions,* the average American eats about twenty teaspoons of refined sugar every day, which is twice the amount recommended by the U.S. Department of Agriculture (ten teaspoons) and four times the maximum recommended by Dr. Dean (five teaspoons a day).[16] No wonder the amount of consumed sugar is so high when one soda pop provides from ten to twenty teaspoons of sugar. Since nutritional balance is crucial for your health, the ideal scenario would be to find a nutritionally oriented physician, dietician, or health professional that could help you suggest a balanced diet with vitamin and mineral supplements.

THE REST OF JERRY'S STORY

After I gave the aforementioned nutritional information to Jerry, I challenged him to change his eating and lifestyle habits. Since I figured it would be hard for Jerry to change something that he had done for so long, I challenged him to try it for one week. Like most people, if you really want something bad enough you will work hard enough to get it. Jerry admitted his incentive at first was to get his wife off his back, but little did he know what would happen. To help Jerry succeed, he took the one-week challenge with an evaluation after that week to see how he felt. I challenged Jerry to do the following:

- No soda pop or other beverage with high sugar content. (Soda pop dehydrates the body, can cause mood swings, sleep disturbance, and poor brain functioning.)

- Drink large amounts of water each day. (Water hydrates the body, improves brain functioning, attention, and concentration.)

- Three meals a day with no "fast foods." (Balanced amounts of proteins and carbohydrates provide adequate fuel for the mind and body, keeps the blood sugar balanced, and can help stabilize moods.)

- Eat no pasta or bread that contains white or refined flour. (Bleached flour has little nutritional value, raises blood sugar, and can cause mood changes.)

- Eat whole wheat or multigrain flour and bread. (Unbleached flour has more nutritional value and helps keep blood sugars balanced.)

- Take a daily vitamin supplement with natural ingredients.

- Exercise two to three times per week (walking, jogging, biking riding, swimming, et cetera. Exercise produces chemicals that elevate moods, improves daily energy level, and improves brain functioning.)

When Jerry came into my office one week later, he looked different. There was more of a bounce in his step with an increased ability to be attentive in our conversation. He slept better at night, concentrated better, and was less tired during the day. Jerry realized he had been playing Russian roulette with his life. He was his own worst enemy, slowly dying inside from lack of nutrition. Jerry was not out of the woods yet. It was still hard for him to give up the things that tasted so good or were so convenient, but the small changes did prove to him that he could feel better. The best part of it all was that he could start controlling what he did with his life, and it was easier to control how he felt physically and emotionally. He admitted it felt good to think better, feel better, and have more energy.

Adequate nutrition is essential for proper functioning of your mental, emotional, and physical health. More specifically, sufficient nutrition is a prerequisite to sustain an emotional connection in any relationship. If you physically feel weak and lethargic, you will not care how you or your partner feels. The amount of energy you put into a relationship will only be as good as the emotional and physical energy you have to give. Changing your eating habits and lifestyle may be among the hardest changes you need to make. However, whether you want to feel better and want a better relationship is entirely up to you. No one can force you to change. However, your life will not improve until you do make a change. These changes are obtainable, and best of all, you have control over the effort you put into it and the results you get out of it.

DEPRESSION

According to the National Institute of Mental Health (NIMH), depressive disorders affect approximately 19 million American adults. For each person directly suffering, their relatives, employees, associates, and friends will also be adversely affected. Depression can interfere with normal functioning and frequently causes problems with work, social, and family adjustment. Fortunately, depression is treatable and significant improvement can be made with the proper help.[17]

According to the NIMH, a depressive disorder is an illness that involves the body, mood, and thoughts. A depressive disorder is not the same as a passing blue mood. It is not a sign of personal weakness or a condition that can be willed or wished away. People with a depressive illness cannot merely "pull themselves together" and get better. Without treatment, symptoms can last for weeks, months, or years. Appropriate treatment can significantly help people who suffer from many of the following symptoms during depression:

- Persistent sad, anxious, or "empty" mood
- Frequent feelings of hopelessness, pessimism, guilt, worthlessness, helplessness
- Loss of interest or pleasure in activities that were once enjoyed, including sex
- Decreased energy, fatigue, being "slowed down"
- Difficulty concentrating, remembering, making decisions
- Insomnia, early-morning awakening, or oversleeping
- Appetite and/or weight loss or overeating and weight gain
- Thoughts of death, thoughts of suicide, or suicide attempts
- Restlessness, irritability
- Persistent physical symptoms that do not respond to treatment, such as headaches, digestive disorders, and chronic pain

REASONS FOR DEPRESSION

Some types of depression run in families, suggesting an inherited chemical imbalance or a negative home environment as the origin. In some families, depressive symptoms also occur generation after generation where your home feels like there is a dark cloud hanging over head with a parent who is routinely sad, pessimistic, negative, angry, or critical. Living in this type of home can create an internal pessimism that becomes a way of life.

Jenny grew up in a home where her mother spent frequent periods in her bedroom away from the family. Jenny could not remember having much fun with mom and did not understand until adulthood that her mother suffered from depression. Jenny learned early in life to keep her feelings and thoughts to herself, in fear she would upset her mother. Her father's frequent words of caution, such as," Don't get your mother upset," reinforced the need to live in silence. Jenny remembered her home as a sad place, filled with a thick heaviness, where people were not happy and laughter was infrequent. As Jenny recalled her childhood, she began to understand why she had a hard time having fun or feeling good about life. She realized she did not learn how to express feelings in childhood and was not able to enjoy life.

TRAUMA, STRESS, AND DEPRESSION

Becoming unemotional can be the result of a traumatic event or emotionally stressful situation. The stress from medical, physical, financial, or emotional hardships can be traumatic enough to bring on a state of depression. However, what makes these situations worse is when a loved one does not provide physical or emotional support. The disappointment from the mate not "being there" can be worse that the incident. While Phil and Leslie sat in my office, Phil was slowly shaking his head from side to side, as if in a daze as he told me about his situation. "I don't know what to do," he said in desperation. Leslie said she couldn't take it anymore and wanted to leave the marriage. "Leslie doesn't talk about her feelings, and I don't know what to say to change her mind," Phil said in a frustrating tone of voice.

I asked Leslie when she could remember the first time she shut down her feelings toward Phil. Leslie sat in silence searching for the right words. Her eyes started watering as if something ugly just surfaced in her memory. She said with a sad whimpering voice, "When Phil wasn't there for me when the doctor told me the bad news." That particular day Phil did not want to accompany Leslie to the doctor's office. In a sudden outburst of hurt, Leslie cried out toward Phil, "I was all alone! Why weren't you there for me?" Although it had been seven years since this incident, Leslie poured out her heart as if it had happened only yesterday. Old hurts pushed deep inside eventually shut you down emotionally, causing a slow death in your relationship.

DEPRESSION IN MEN AND WOMEN

Women experience depression about twice as often as men. One reason is that women tend to be able to identify and express their feelings about depression better than men. Also many hormonal factors may contribute to the increased rate of depression in women, particularly such factors as menstrual cycle changes, pregnancy, miscarriage, postpartum period, premenopause, and menopause. Many women also face additional stresses such as responsibilities at work and home, single parenthood, or caring for children and aging parents at the same time. On the positive side, women tend to have less medical problems and live longer (compared to men) because they let emotions out.

Although statistics show men are less likely to suffer from depression than women, men are less likely to admit to depression, and doctors are less likely to suspect it. However, the holding in of emotions may be a contributing factor to the climbing rate of suicide (four times higher in men than in women). A man's depression is often masked by alcohol, drugs, or working long hours. Depression typically shows up in men not as feelings of hopelessness and helplessness, but as being irritable, angry, and discouraged. Hence, depression may be more difficult to recognize in men. Even if a man realizes that he is depressed, he may be less willing to seek help. Encouragement and support from concerned family members can make a difference for both men and women.

TREATMENT FOR DEPRESSION

If symptoms of depression interfere with normal life activities, it would be advisable to seek help. Here are some suggestions:

- Have a medical examination from a physician to rule out any problems that may be causing the symptoms.
- Change any dietary or nutritional deficiencies. Seek help from a nutritionally minded health professional.
- Pray specifically for healing from the depression and seek prayer support from others.
- Seek counseling to understand the symptoms, find the causes, learn how to eliminate those causes, and learn how to deal with depression.
- Exercise regularly. Find time to relax, become involved with positive minded people, church fellowship, Bible study, and/or prayer group.

If symptoms are left untreated, the depression can become severe with an inability to function at work, home, or with your family. When this occurs, an evaluation with a medical physician, counselor, or psychiatrist may be advised for medication or other avenues of treatment.

Personal Reflection

May I become more aware of how I feel in my body and in my heart, and may God give me the wisdom and strength to take proper care of both.

STUDY QUESTIONS

1. Describe how you take care of your mind, body, and soul. (How do you eat, sleep, exercise, and pray?)

2. What can you do to make healthy changes to take better care of yourself?

3. Describe any symptoms that suggest you are experiencing depression.

4. Describe what may be potential causes for depression.

5. What can you do to make healthy changes to treat the depression?

6. After reading this chapter, what additional insights have you learned about yourself and what can you do to change your life or your situation for the better?

11

YOUR HEALTH AFFECTS
HOW YOU THINK

~

If you keep doing what you've always done,
you'll always get what you've always gotten.
—John C. Maxwell

If you recall the story about Jerry from the last chapter, you will remember he did not sleep well, complained of feeling blah, and was tired throughout the day. Well, there was more to his story. Jerry stated that his wife, Linda, usually complained he did not pay attention during conversations and showed little interest in doing things with her. Jerry wondered if his racing thoughts and difficulty concentrating had anything to do with not being able to have a good conversation with his wife. I told Jerry, poor energy, a racing mind, and poor concentration were ingredients that would make conversations and close relationships very difficult for anyone. Let's explore the conditions of sleep deprivation, Attention Deficit Disorder, and substance abuse and see how these conditions can adversely affect you and your relationship.

SLEEP DEPRIVATION

You go to bed tired and wake up tired. You have to pull yourself out of bed and have a cup of coffee just to wake up. You may drag yourself through the day, but you still work long hours into the evening, live life to the fullest, or become too busy to find time for adequate rest. So common is the difficulty of getting sufficient sleep that the medical community has labeled it "Sleep Deprivation." It is more common in Type-A personalities, single parents, mothers working outside the home, and people working second and third shifts. The net results of not getting enough sleep are impaired judgment, diminished creativity and productivity, inability to concentrate, reduced language and communication skills, slowed reaction times, and decreased abilities to learn and remember.[18]

For people living a lifestyle with less sleep, their minds and bodies have become conditioned to function with less. You think, react, and feel at a reduced state of functioning, even to a state of numbness, as if you are impaired mentally, physically, and emotionally. Recent research has verified that chronic poor sleep results in daytime tiredness, difficulties with focused attention, low threshold to express negative emotion (irritability and easily frustrated), and difficulty . . . [regulating] emotions.[19] Life can be so busy that you don't let yourself notice how tired you really feel. The loss of sleep creates a sense of apathy in which you have little energy to perform tasks and little desire to express emotion. You also have less patience with others who generate conflict or demand your time.

As a sleep-deprived person, you may believe you are working hard for the sake of the family. However, it is often the case that the amount of time away from the home usually leaves little time for the family. The constant requests from the family to give them more time only creates resentment because you are already stretched too thin. The hurt and resentment among family members only serves to increase the lack of understanding and poor communication between everyone.

CHANGING YOUR LIFESTYLE

In order for me not to come across like your spouse (or your mother), I will be plain and simple. Sleep deprivation will destroy your life and hurt your family. Although you probably can give me a good reason for living this way, the reason will not matter if you are not around to talk about it or your family will not wait around to hear about it. If you don't do something now, your health and family situation will only get worse. Give yourself permission to take care of yourself by getting more sleep and better nutrition.

Let's think outside the box. Think of the purpose of your lifestyle and who it benefits. Determine your priorities, i.e., what is absolutely necessary and what you can let go. There is usually a reason why you must work so hard and/or cannot organize your priorities enough to give room for yourself, your family, or God. Since lack of sleep may be from a variety of causes, it would be very important to receive a medical examination from a nutritionally mindful physician to rule out any medical or physical problems. Some other culprits for poor sleep are: sleep apnea, depression, stressful occupation or lifestyle, medication side effects, obesity, and poor diet. Stop consuming large amounts of carbohydrates (bread, pasta, and cakes), sugar, salt [sodium], or drinks with caffeine during the evening (before bed). Seek counseling to help change how you live and think. Find time to relax, pray, and spend time with your family.

ATTENTION DEFICIT HYPERACTIVITY DISORDER

There is an increasingly common condition called, ADHD (Attention-Deficit/Hyperactivity Disorder) or ADD (Attention Deficit Disorder without hyperactivity) that affects the mind and body. Some professionals believe that ADHD or ADD are conditions wherein an individual's brain cannot slow down enough to stay on task, comprehend, or express thoughts and feelings. If the condition is not treated in childhood, you grow into adulthood adjusting your thinking and lifestyle to compensate for the difficulties. Recent research has verified that chronic poor sleep results in daytime tiredness, difficulties with focused attention, low threshold to express negative emotion (irritability and easily frustrated), and difficulty [regulating] emotions. These are the same symptoms that can earn kids (and adults) the diagnosis of Attention Deficit Hyperactivity Disorder.[20] Both ADD and ADHD have the following similar characteristics in adults:

- Poor attention span. Easily distracted or has a hard time following directions, leaves tasks unfinished, doesn't listen or loses things often.

- Impatient, acts and speaks without thinking

- Unable to stay focused on a conversation. Poor communicator of feelings and thoughts. May talk too much or hold in feelings until there is a blow up of emotion.

- Easily agitated. May have anger outbursts.

- In the case of ADHD the individual has hyperactivity (i.e., always full of energy).

Since the lack of attention span often makes it difficult to have normal conversations and be mindful of daily responsibilities, this condition can have devastating affects on your relationship. Even remembering to pick up the kids or returning phone calls can become a major point of aggravation for the family. Your emotional mate has a right to become aggravated when he or she is trying to discuss something important and you are off in another world. Every time you forget or you don't listen your mate feels like you don't care. Your emotional mate needs to learn and be reminded repeatedly that the ADD partner is not intentionally trying to hurt or ignore others. The ADD person cannot help the fact that his or her mind is going in so many directions and has difficulty focusing on one thing for a long period of time.

If you have lived with ADD all your life, you have adapted your thinking and behaviors to live this way. After hearing complaints all your life, you develop an underlying feeling of failure and poor self confidence that are a common response to living with the ADD condition. Since it can be a struggle to live in a world where you do not think and feel the same as others, you learned to shut out, tune out, walk out, or yell out what you feel. The exact cause for ADD is unknown but many natural health physicians and researchers believe that potential causes for the modern epidemic of ADHD and ADD may include a combination of the following: food additives, poor diet, low blood sugar, refined sugar, allergies (especially to food), genetic predisposition, thyroid dysfunction, chemical imbalance, vaccinations, formaldehyde, damage to the brain from an injury, excess stress at birth, and mineral deficiency.

HELPING A PERSON WITH ADHD OR ADD

Don't settle with a belief that you must "suffer" with either ADHD or ADD the rest of your life. There are too many options that can help. Do not settle for only one professional opinion, no matter how many letters there are after their name. There is more literature, web sites, seminars, even clinics devoted to the treatment of ADD and ADHD than any one person can know. It is my hope that you learn as much as you can about the symptoms and treatment of this condition. Qualified professionals, including a medical physician (MD or DO), naturopathic physician (NMD or ND), experienced mental health therapist, and/or psychologist can help begin various forms of treatment. A combination of treatments may include:

- Medical examination to rule out any physical or allergy problems that may be contributing to the symptoms.

- Change any dietary or nutritional deficiencies. Seek help from a nutritionally minded health professional.

- Counseling for emotional and family issues.

- Prescription medications can be helpful.

- Alternative treatments, such as physical or sensory exercises and natural remedies have been very successful in reducing or eliminating symptoms.

SUBSTANCES THAT AFFECT YOUR EMOTION

Doris's face became tight with anger as she voiced her frustration about her husband, Frank. When I asked for more details, Doris threw up her hands to emphasize her disgust, "When he starts drinking, I can't talk to him. He's like another person." Doris continued, "I've told him how much it bothers me when he drinks, but he says it makes him relax. He just doesn't care." As Doris shared her stories of intense arguments, tears of frustration, loneliness, and desires to give up, it didn't surprise me that she was emotionally at the end of her rope. She felt there was no emotional connection, as if her husband was in another world most of the time.

Doris's situation is very common among couples where one partner is negatively affected from using substances such as illegal drugs, alcohol, or excessive amounts of prescription drugs. I am not referring to people that properly use medications for medical or mental health conditions. I am referring to people like Frank who use substances as a way to get through life. For example, using alcohol as a way to relax is a red flag that shows either life has gotten out of hand or you never learned how to deal with the stress of life. Either way, if you use substances to get through life, you are not living in reality; you act differently, just ask your mate. If you believe you express yourself better when you drink, you are only fooling yourself. That is a common misconception. The truth is you were born with the ability to express your feelings. The fact that you must use a drug to open your mind is a huge indicator you have some issues to be healed. Like many people, you may be using substances to escape, hide, tolerate, or have "fun" in a world you cannot handle. Ironically, the very substance you use to escape life will eventually be the next problem in life you will need to escape.

Any time you use substances that alter your mind, the ability to emotionally connect is destroyed and the relationship is undermined at the very core. If your mate has repeatedly requested you to stop using substances, your continued use of a substance is interpreted as a betrayal of your love or a sign you do not care about the relationship. This destroys the trust that holds the relationship together. The substance user will not change unless they will lose something more important than the substance they are using.

HELP FOR THE SUBSTANCE USER

If you think you need a substance to enjoy life or to handle the ups and downs of the day, you have a problem. You first must admit you have a problem and get help to change. Here are some suggestions:

- Pray for deliverance from the ugly grip and ask others to help you give it up.

- Seek counseling.

- Change your lifestyle, i.e., do not spend time with others or attend places that offer the substance with which you have a problem.

- Attend a support group, i.e., Alcoholic or Narcotics Anonymous.

- If you are a mate who is living with a substance user and you have asked and pleaded for them to stop with no permanent change, you need to change your approach. I will address what you can do differently in later chapters.

WORDS OF ENCOURAGEMENT

If you relate with any of this chapter, you should not settle for the state of mind or body in which you are living. You were created with the intent to live life to the fullest by utilizing the body, mind, and emotions you were born with. You need to take care of the body you were given. You need to treat your body with the same respect that you would want others to treat you. You do not need to make the changes alone. Allow others to help find answers. The next chapter will help you put all this information together.

Personal Reflection
May I take care of my body with wisdom and maturity,
knowing it is the only body I will have.

≈

STUDY QUESTIONS

1. Describe any symptoms that suggest you are experiencing sleep deprivation.

2. What can you do to make healthy changes to treat the sleep deprivation?

3. Describe any symptoms that suggest you are experiencing ADD or ADHD.

4. What can you do to make healthy changes to treat the ADD or ADHD?

5. Describe any symptoms that suggest you are negatively affected by substances.

6. What can you do to make healthy changes to treat the substance using?

7. After reading this chapter, what additional insights have you learned about yourself and what can you do to change your life for the better?

PART III

making changes

12

DETERMINE WHAT
NEEDS TO CHANGE

~

Unhealthy people create unhealthy relationships.
Heal the people and you heal the relationship.

When you have many unresolved wounds from the past and combine them with poor diet, sleep deprivation, depression, ADD, and harmful substances, you have the greatest potential to live an unemotional life. However, life does not need to continue this way. Making changes is very possible for the person who *wants* to change. You should be encouraged that you have come this far. Let's keep going to make changes.

DETERMINING WHAT YOU NEED TO CHANGE

If you have been unemotional all your life, you may have not tried to make changes because you did not know what to change or how to change. Often, the hardest part for the unemotional person is admitting that he or she needs to make a change. However, if you do not like living this way, the only thing getting in the way of feeling and thinking better is YOU. Start by recognizing what you need to change by filling out this check list.

The UNEMOTIONAL MATE can complete the following check list to determine what is applicable to his or her life:

_____1. Have symptoms of depression.

____2. Have symptoms of sleep deprivation.

____3. Have symptoms of ADD or ADHD.

____4. On a regular basis, do not feel physically fit or energetic.

____5. Childhood includes adults that were unemotional.

____6. See life more in extremes—black or white.

____7. Unable to emotionally respond or validate the feelings of others.

____8. Have a difficult time finding the words to communicate feelings.

____9. Childhood includes emotional/physical/sexual hurtful experiences.

____10. Sex is what makes me feel emotionally close to my mate rather than finding an emotional connection through regular hugs and kisses.

____11. My emotions are so closed down that I find no desire for sexual intimacy in my relationship.

____12. I become emotionally upset or shut down when I do not get my way or others do not agree.

The EMOTIONAL MATE and family members can complete the following check list to determine what is applicable to the unemotional person:

____1. See symptoms of depression.

____2. See symptoms of sleep deprivation.

____3. See symptoms of ADD or ADHD.

____4. On a regular basis, he or she does not feel physically fit or energetic.

_____5. His or her childhood includes adults that were un-emotional.

_____6. His or her childhood includes emotional/physical/sexual hurtful experiences.

_____7. He or she is unable to emotionally respond or validate the feelings of others.

_____8. He or she has a difficult time finding the words to communicate feelings.

_____9. He or she sees life more in extremes—black or white.

_____10. Sex is what makes him or her feel emotionally close rather than finding an emotional connection through regular hugs and kisses.

_____11. His or her emotions are closed down and there is no time of sexual intimacy in the relationship.

_____12. He or she becomes emotionally upset or shut down when he or she does not get their way or others do not agree.

After both lists are checked:

- The areas that have been checked (on both lists) will determine what needs to be changed. To obtain a more accurate view of the issues, the checked areas on both lists need to be considered.

- Information to help you: For numbers checked one through four, there is helpful information in chapters ten and eleven. For numbers checked five through twelve, there is helpful information in chapters seventeen through twenty-one.

RECOGNIZE WHY YOU WANT TO CHANGE

When the unemotional person is motivated to make

changes, it will be more difficult to move forward if the attempts to change are for the wrong reason. The unemotional person must want to change because they personally want to improve their own life rather than trying to please someone else. Let me explain this in more detail with the following examples.

1. **Are you motivated to change because of a person or circumstance?**

Change will take place only when you want to change for yourself and not for someone else. If you are deciding to change because of pressures from your spouse or to save the relationship, then you may be doomed to fail. In other words, if you are changing for someone or the relationship, you are trying to conform to what you believe that person expects of you. As a result, your motivation to change is dependent upon the response of that person and the outcome of the relationship rather than relying on the motivation from your own personal belief that you need to change. For example, if the relationship is going well, there is a belief you have "arrived," and there is less of a need to work on change. Or, if your mate does not react the way you expect (or want), there is a belief you are being disrespected, triggering your reaction to stop working on the change. Here is an example where the wrong motivation leads to disaster.

Martha ran off to the bedroom after Jay fired hurtful words that pierced her heart for the thousandth time. In the midst of it all, Martha threatened to leave if Jay didn't make changes. Martha was extremely unhappy with the way she has been treated over the years and vowed to make some changes in herself. For the next two weeks, Jay began his usual "nice husband" routine by becoming remorseful for his barrage of hurtful words. He helped around the house, helped with the kids, and acted nicer than usual. However, this was the first time Martha had stopped any cooking, talking, or intimate contact with Jay, which made him realize things were more serious than usual. Jay tried to impress Martha with his nice husband routine by giving more money to spend on a dress and staying home from a night out with the guys.

Everything was going well until Martha said it was too early to decide whether she was going to stay in the relationship. When Jay heard that comment, he burst out in anger, "I'm making all these changes and you don't care about me. Why do I bother to try?" Jay's acts of kindness were only temporary since his motivation to change came from his wife's threat to leave, not from his own belief that he needed to change. In addition, Jay looked to the actions and moods of Martha as his indicator to determine whether he had changed enough. For example, if Martha looked happy, Jay interpreted that as he was doing things right. If Martha was not happy, he would respond by throwing up his hands in defense, saying, "What's the use?" Jay believed he was making an earnest effort to change but became agitated when Martha did not appreciate the changes he attempted. Jay's motivation to change was to please Martha, instead of acknowledging his need to look at his own issues and need to change for himself. Each time Martha accepted Jay's apology in the past, he would eventually do something hurtful again. Martha felt miserable living this way and believed Jay was playing mind games. Each time this pattern happened, Martha became more cautious about letting her guard down.

2. **Does your motivation to change come from realizing you need to personally alter your life to be different than what it has been, no matter what anyone says or does?**

This motivation is based on your awareness that you have a problem and a personal conviction that you need to be different. You are willing to make changes regardless of the pressure, demands, or expectations of someone else or some circumstance. Your motivation comes from an internal belief that the long-term outcome of becoming a better person is worth more than the short-term gains of trying to impress your spouse. As a result, you are more likely to follow through with the change regardless of the intentions of someone else or any circumstances, no matter how unpleasant they may be. Let's continue with the story of Jay and Martha as an example.

Over time, Jay's selfish, hurtful attitude became worse, which only gained him divorce papers and a swift boot out of the house. After one month of separation, Jay showed up in my office with a look that could win depressed face of the year. "I can't believe this is happening," he said while trying to hold back tears that had been held inside for weeks. He continued, as if he was finally confessing something, "One minute I'm mad because she did this to me; the next minute I'm afraid this is the end of everything." Jay didn't have any trouble holding back his anger toward Martha, "I want to strike back before I lose everything," he said in a tone of resentment. Over the next few weeks, as that anger decreased, Jay realized his motivation for change did not work and he needed to drastically change his attitude.

In counseling, he recognized that he never had a lasting, close, loving relationship with a woman. (This included his mother and girlfriends.) It became painfully clear he had to make personal changes if a healthy relationship was ever going to be a reality. Jay recognized he needed to stop trying to get even with his wife and focus his intentions on changing his own emotional issues and selfish attitude. Regardless how Martha reacted toward him, Jay realized his motivation to change needed to come from the belief that he needed to personally take responsibility to alter his life, no matter what happened to the marriage. If he tried to change for Martha, then he would blame his wife if she did not act like he expected. He needed to take responsibility for his own actions and not blame the consequences of his actions or the deterioration of the marriage on others. Ironically, Jay's inability to develop and maintain loving relationships was the very problem he blamed on everyone else. Jay realized he needed to identify and heal his hurting emotions from past relationships before he could learn to deal with the hurt he felt with his current relationship.

RECOGNIZE YOU CANNOT CHANGE ON YOUR OWN

Whether you are the unemotional person or living with the unemotional person, it is the intention of this book to provide information to give you ideas on how to carry through the process of change. Everyone going through this type of situation can benefit from the help that God, a counselor, friends, and family can bring to your situation.

1. **Allowing God into the healing process**

In your quest to find healing, look to the promises that God brings according to Psalm 30:2, "O Lord my God, I called to you for help and you healed me." You or anyone else will not know exactly when and where that healing will take place, but God wants to help you find that healing. In order for permanent life change, there needs to be an alteration of the heart. You can only transform your life when you recognize you have a way of life that needs to change and you want to change, no matter what any other person says or does. Until you acknowledge you have a difficulty with expressing emotions and emotionally relating with others, you will have difficulty changing. Write this prayer on a card and pray every day from your heart:

*Dear Lord, give me a new heart and put a new
spirit in me; remove my heart of stone and give me
a heart of flesh. (Ezekiel 36:26 Paraphrased)*

2. Allow a counselor into the healing process

Over the years I have repeatedly heard the stories of frustration from both the unemotional person and the emotional mate who have experienced little change after numerous counseling attempts. Basically, traditional counseling such as "psychotherapy" or "talk therapy" will encourage you to tell your story as the therapist asks questions such as "How do you feel," "Telling me how that affected you," etc. If you are unemotional, you will not be able to relate to those questions. Traditional talk therapy can be effective for most people needing counseling, but it is not effective for people who are emotionally stuck. This is NOT an excuse for you to skip talking to a counselor. Rather, it is a recommendation to find a counselor that is experienced in working with people that have a history of being unemotional.

It would be ideal to find a mental health professional who is experienced with working in the areas of nutritional supplements, depression, sleep deprivation, and ADD. If you cannot find one professional that can treat everything, find additional professionals to help with those areas. Make sure each professional is aware of what the other is doing by signing a Release of Information form and requesting the professionals to speak with each other to coordinate your care. It is smart to seek wise counsel for anything you have difficulty accomplishing on your own, especially godly counsel. Proverbs 15:22 states, "Plans fail for lack of counsel, but with many advisors they succeed." See the appendix for details about finding a counselor.

3. Find support from other sources

This is not a time to try changing everything all by yourself.

Emotional, spiritual, physical, social, and financial help from others may be necessary to move forward with change. During your journey toward healing, allow others to help. Reach out to family members, friends, church members, a counselor, or support group to find encouragement and direction. Even writing your thoughts in a daily journal can be helpful.

WORDS OF ENCOURAGEMENT

Although it took you a long time to develop these issues, it will take less time to change them if you are determined to change. Remember that change is a process, not like a light switch. Your patience may wear thin as you work through these changes, but allow yourself to take one step at a time and frequently look back to where you started to see where you have grown. Find strength in knowing that God's grace is sufficient for you, for His power is made perfect in weakness. You can boast all the more gladly about your weakness so that Christ's power may rest on you, (2 Corinthians 12:9 paraphrased). When you are at your weakest, is where you need to let God work at His best to help you.

Remember to use this personal reflection daily

Dear Lord, give me a new heart and put the Holy Spirit in me; remove my heart of stone and give me a heart of flesh.

(Ezekiel 36:26 paraphrased)

STUDY QUESTIONS

1. What areas did the checklist indicate you need to address in your life?

2. Are you motivated to change because of a person or circumstance? Explain.

3. Does your motivation for change come from realizing you need to be different than how you have been, no matter what anyone says or does? Explain.

4. How will you allow God into the healing process?

5. How will you allow a professional into the healing process?

6. What support can you find from other sources to help you with the change?

7. After reading this chapter, what additional insights have you learned about yourself and what else can you do to change your life for the better?

13

WHEN "LETTING GO" OF THE PAST DOESN'T WORK

~

Problems in life will only get worse
if you ignore the lessons from them.

Anna was driving home tired from a busy day. Trying to break up the boring ride, she turns on the radio, which tunes into a speaker she's heard before. At that moment, the speaker was finishing a statement about coping with the problems of life. "The past is in the past, and you need to live for the present," the speaker said with conviction in his voice. Anna began to focus on his every word, "Take those old thoughts and give them away to God," he continued. Anna's blood pressure began to rise, as she continued to listen. "You don't need to hold onto it anymore; it's in the past. Just let it go."

Anna quickly reached down in frustration and shut off the radio. "I don't get it," she said, as if she were talking to the speaker, "I know I have some issues still inside, but I can't seem to get rid of them. Even when I ask God to take them away, the same old hurts keep coming up." Anna stared at the cars in front of her as she said with sadness, "Why can't I just get rid of these past issues in my life?"

All too often, I hear the frustration of people like Anna, who have the desire to rid their mind and body of unhealthy emotional baggage, but nothing seems to work. Maybe you have been struggling with some emotional issues or have been unemotional for some time and you've been told by some well-meaning friend, doctor, or family member to "just let it go." To make matters worse, maybe you've seen a pastor thumping a Bible as they insist the only way to get right with God is to let go of your past. Maybe there were times you gave the past to God and the issues stopped for a while, only to resurface with an emotional outburst.

If you have been struggling like Anna or you know someone who lives in a life without emotions, it is time to get serious about finding a solution. The next two chapters are primarily for anyone who has been struggling with the following criteria:

1. You have emotional issues (anger, anxiety, fear, etc.) that will not go away or you are an unemotional person that has been unsuccessful at getting in touch with his or her feelings.

2. You have realized few changes after trying everything from ignoring, praying, counseling, medication, reading books, even the church leaders praying over you.

3. You are tired of living this way and ready to try something different.

SUFFERING FROM UNHEALTHY EMOTIONS

Often, the unhealthy emotions (such as anxiety, anger, insomnia, fears, mood swings, etc.) are getting in the way of feeling good about yourself or interfering with maintaining healthy relationships. When you are unemotional or live in a relationship that does not allow feelings, you push away the emotion, denying its existence, hoping those emotional issues will never return. If you are tired of living with unhealthy emotions, it's time to stop pretending you are feeling fine and begin finding permanent healing.

There is a reason why you cannot let go of your emotional baggage, as if there is a lesson to learn or some personal growth to take place. Being unemotional or experiencing unhealthy emotions that will not go away represent unresolved painful experiences in your life that must be healed. The longer you hold in or ignore these unresolved hurts, the more likely you will remain unemotional or suffer from unhealthy emotions.

BUILDING THE WALL

Anna admitted she did not want to come to counseling, but realized how much she was dissatisfied with life. "While sitting home alone one day, it dawned on me how pathetic my life has been," Anna shared as if revealing a deep secret. "For years," Anna continued, "I've felt this dark cloud hanging over me, like a weight or something that I could never put my finger on. I never realized until now that it seemed hard to enjoy life, like I've been fooling myself."

I asked if her husband provided comfort or emotional support when she felt sad or depressed. Anna said, while trying to hold back the tears, "I can't talk about my feelings with my husband. He just makes fun of me or uses them against me. I gave up trying to get emotional support from him a long time ago."

As Anna talked about her past, it was as if a light bulb went on in her head. Until now, she never realized why she could not get close to people or express her emotions. She admitted that the feelings of hurt, rejection, sadness, and loneliness she felt as a child have continued into adulthood, especially in her marriage. From all the hurt caused by the important people in her life, Anna had built a wall to shield her heart from getting hurt again. She now understood that the wall protected her heart from letting anymore hurt get in and did not allow her to "let go" of the hurt held inside.

If you have experienced hurts or trauma in your life and you were not allowed to express your emotions or no one was available to provide emotional support, those emotions would get pushed down inside. If there was no safe way to let them go, it is very common for you to push the feelings aside. I met with David when he was going through a struggling marriage. David explained how difficult it was for him to trust people and feel close to his wife. "It's like our relationship is on a roller coaster ride; we are either arguing or making up."

When I asked him about his childhood, David said he did not have the greatest relationship with his parents. He could talk about some things with his mother but never had a good relationship with his father. As a result of his father's anger outbursts, strict rules, and frequent discipline, David carried feelings of sadness, rejection, fear, and anger throughout his life. David was afraid to express his feelings growing up and was forced to push away those negative feelings deep inside by building a wall around his heart. The wall helped to bury the emotions and shut out any other new hurts that may come along. Unfortunately, David never realized that his wall sealed shut his heart, which was the reason why he could not express his feelings and had difficulty becoming emotionally close to anyone—especially his wife and God.

BUILDING A FORTRESS

When you live with these feelings all your life, you don't know how to live any other way. To protect your heart against additional hurts, you build a wall to make life tolerable and safe in a hurtful world. Like with Anna and David, each new hurt you experience stacks one more layer of bricks on your wall, holding the hurts tightly inside for safe keeping. The wall of bricks and mortar become thicker the longer you hold inside the hurting emotions. Over the years, the wall becomes a fortress, keeping your emotions in and everyone else out. The layers of the fortress can subtly grow brick by brick as you live year after year in an unhealthy relationship or situation. Those bricks can be in the form of emotions such as, resentment, anger, bitterness, disappointment, betrayal, unfaithfulness, fear, guilt, regret, loneliness, and unforgiveness. The very fortress wall that was built to protect your heart, mind, and soul is unfortunately the same fortress wall that prevents you from expressing feelings.

When you live with a wall around your heart, you cannot enjoy life to the fullest because you don't even know what living to the fullest is like. Your relationships tend to be shallow and you have difficulty relating with your feelings because the wall prevents you from going deep enough to really know what you are feeling. Much of the time, you believe you are relating fine, because that is all you know. Deep down you sense the dissatisfaction in your life, but you continue to live in shallow relationships because you do not know any other way. The longer you hold on to those old emotions, resentments, and even unforgiveness, the more the wall becomes impermeable to allowing anyone inside your heart or allowing any change to take place.

Drs. Minirth, Meier, Hemfelt, Sneed and Mr. Hawkins, in their book *Love Hunger* state the following: "When we hold resentment against God, others or ourselves, serotonin and norepinephrine are depleted in our brain cells. These are the chemicals that move across the synapses from one cell to the next, the chemicals that we think with, move with. When these are depleted, people lose energy and motivation."[21] Serotonin is the chemical that boosts your mood. The lower the serotonin level, the more depressed your mood becomes. The unforgiveness and unresolved hurts in your life act as festering open wounds in your heart, mind, and soul that create problems in your emotional, physical, and spiritual areas of life.

The longer you have lived in a fortress, the less likely anyone or anything will be able to penetrate the walls of that fortress. This is usually the reason why you do not allow friends, a mate, God, or counseling to penetrate the thick brick wall that shields the old emotional wounds. That is why you feel like nothing works. Your wall stops you from connecting with anyone, including God. Your wall does not let your feelings out and does not let anyone in. Like Anna, your failed efforts to make changes only generate more frustration and discouragement, creating the belief you are helpless to change what you are told is wrong. Unfortunately, this only makes the wall even thicker.

WORDS OF ENCOURAGEMENT TO PENETRATE THE WALL

If you are living with a thick brick wall around your heart, the objective is to get inside and recover the treasure of your heart. However, you may ask, "If I've already tried everything, how can I get inside the wall," (without using the dynamite that your mate would suggest)? For the unemotional person with the characteristics described in this book, there is no traditional medicine of which I am aware that breaks down the thick wall. Antidepressant medication can be used to raise your spirits when depression coincides with living an emotionless life. The down side is that the antidepressant can also serve to mask your real emotions, giving you the false belief that everything is "fine." If the unemotional person believes everything is fine, he or she will not seek professional help, no matter what the emotional partner says or does. Traditional psychotherapy, talk therapy, and many alternative therapies that utilize feelings as the primary entry point for treatment have poor results of penetrating the fortress wall. Often, people do not have enough patience, insurance, or money to wait out the length of time it can take with these traditional treatments. As a result, you need to change how you think about emotional healing by using what is naturally provided to help penetrate that wall. The next chapter will help you change how you think about emotional healing.

Personal Reflection
May I recognize the wall and reveal the truth
about my emotions held inside.

STUDY QUESTIONS

1. Describe any unhealthy emotions or behaviors in your life (or someone you know) of which you cannot let go?

2. If there is a wall around your heart, describe what emotions or hurts that wall may be made from.

3. In what ways have you or others tried to penetrate that wall?

4. After reading this chapter, what additional insights have you learned about yourself and what can you do to change your life for the better?

14

NATURAL SOLUTIONS TO HEAL THE HEART & MIND

~

*"Fruit trees of all kinds will grow on both banks
of the river . . . Their fruit will serve for food and
their leaves for healing,"* (Ezekiel 47:12)

*Thus, behind all disease lie our fears, our anxiet-
ies, our greed, our likes and our dislikes. Let us
seek these out, heal them, and with the healing of
them will go the disease from which we suffer.*
—Dr. Edward Bach, *The Twelve Healers*

By the time people living in emotionless relationships come to my office, they often feel they are on the edge of a cliff barely holding on by their fingers tips (if they have not fallen off already). If you have been searching and praying for answers and not experienced much change, there is a great sense of frustration and helplessness, as if people and God have let you down. If you are in this type of situation, do not despair. God is still in the business of healing and there are people still interested in helping your situation. If you have tried praying, counseling, and traditional medication without much success, the following is one natural alternative that has been found to heal unhealthy emotions that are locked deep inside.

HEALING THROUGH HOMEOPATHY

By now, you should know the longer an unemotional mate buries suppressed emotions behind a wall, the more difficult it will be to have a healthy relationship. In addition, the longer an emotional mate lives in an emotionless relationship, the more likely they will also bury emotions behind a wall. However, one natural and safe way to break down the wall is through the healing of homeopathy. This two hundred year old natural form of healing is a very safe, user-friendly, and not habit forming treatment, that is derived from plant, animal, and mineral extracts. It works naturally within the mind and body to break down the unhealthy walls by dissolving emotion held deep inside. Homeopathy was introduced in America in the 1820s, and by the turn of the century, up to 25% of all medical doctors practiced this form of treatment. By the 1920s, homeopathy decreased for many reasons such as the introduction of the new fast-acting, cure-all drugs such as antibiotics. However, homeopathy has steadily become very popular over the years, as people are demanding forms of treatment that are healthier, safer, less costly, and give better results.

This is good news for anyone who needs to penetrate a brick wall that blocks emotion or for any person with unhealthy emotions (i.e., anger, hurt) that will not go away. This is also good news for the emotional mate who is hurting as a result of living with the unemotional mate. In his book, *Homeopathic Medicine For Mental Health,* Trevor Smith, M.D. states the homeopathic remedy "has the ability to liberate vital energies locked up in the body, so that a healthier self is experienced, with a greater sense of vitality, energy and well-being."[22] Dr. Smith continues by writing, the homeopathic remedy "helps lessen the denial of painful hurts and memories, which can then be more easily brought to the surface, recalled, understood and discussed. This quite naturally leads to a strengthening of the personality, confidence and greater insights. Being able to tolerate mixed feelings, previously thought impossible...."[23]

Suppressed emotions from old traumas, hurts, and disappointments are held in flesh, cells, muscles, tendons, posture, organs, and memories. Homeopathic remedies work by stimulating the immune system, the tensions, distortions, and memories to gradually release the old wounds like peeling the layers of an onion. As the layers of hurt are naturally released, the mind and soul find more clarity, which you experience when feeling like your old self again or feeling a calm and contentment never felt before.

If the unemotional characteristics are the result of unresolved wounds, they will most likely be suppressed in the form of layers. These layers are packed tightly deep inside, unrecognizable to the unemotional person. Peter Chappell, in his book *Emotional Healing with Homoeopathy*, describes a person's life like a river flowing from the vitality of the soul. Somewhere in your life there is a dam, "created by wrongly processed and stored feelings, so that the flow is dammed up and overflowing the banks." The author continues with the good news, "Fortunately homeopathic remedies are like road maps of all known human malfunctions, so one can be found to release the dam, the constriction, and it will be washed away. Initially there will be an increased flow, carrying along with it a lot of debris from the dam and what was accumulated behind it. This is the toxic elimination process which commonly occurs after taking a homeopathic remedy. Then equilibrium will be restored, all the people living alongside the river will calm down and a sense of peace and harmony will return."[24]

BREAKING THE WALL DOWN

A person can deal with unhealthy emotions primarily in two different ways. You can become unemotional from suppressed emotions, similar to the example of David in the previous chapter or by experiencing unhealthy emotions that will not go away, similar to the example of Anna also found in the previous chapter. The homeopathic remedy can be used to treat David and Anna by knocking down the brick wall and allowing the natural flow of energy to free the mind and body of the emotion. For example, Anna's emotional and physical symptoms fit the homeopathic remedy called Ignatia. This remedy was suggested for the grief and sadness she has held inside over the last twenty years from the important relationships she lost. The first few days Anna took Ignatia she began experiencing symptoms that represented the releasing of old emotion. She dreamed of old memories, felt sadness, and experienced occasional tears that would come and go. Over a period of a few weeks, she felt less depressed and was less irritable. As she continued this remedy, Anna experienced more mental clarity, an increased sense of confidence, felt happier, and she did not feel as burdened when daily problems came up. Each time she released emotion, she would feel physically relaxed and emotionally freer, as one more layer of bricks came off the wall.

CONVENTIONAL MEDICINE VS. HOMEOPATHIC REMEDIES

You may wonder, if these treatments are so great, why doctors do not talk about them. You need to know that conventional medicine and homeopathic remedies are two different forms or schools of treatment. "Conventional medicine generally aims at treating the physical effects of the traumas without recognizing or giving attention to the underlying causes, believing in essence that all disease is physical."[25] "Homeopathic remedies by comparison 'mimic' inner traumas: they 'remind' the body to 'unstick and resolve' them so that they can naturally dissolve themselves."[26] Homeopathic "treatment is free from the often disastrous side-effects of the typical allopathic [traditional medicine] prescription, and when the treatment is stopped, the patient does not slide back to his previous state of illness. Homeopathic patients hold their gains, and are not dependent upon their pills once they have made an initial improvement."[27]

Even though you can obtain homeopathic remedies through retail health food stores, you are strongly recommended to see a professional, experienced in administering *mental health* homeopathic remedies, to determine just the right remedy for you. A professional knowledgeable in homeopathy can select the right remedy by obtaining past and present personal information to identify emotion/physical issues that need to be treated. These remedies are for anyone wanting to be free of unhealthy emotions but do not want to deal with the side effects typically found in other forms of medicine.

WORDS OF ENCOURAGEMENT

I strongly recommend you begin working with a counselor with some years of experience in the areas of which you must let go. If your feelings are blocked and therapy does not progress after a short period of time, you may want to either change therapists or find a professional (i.e., medical doctor, chiropractor, nutritionist, mental health counselor, and naturopathic physician, and homeopath) with experience in homeopathic mental health remedies to work with your counselor. It is very important that homeopathic remedies and counseling not become a replacement for prayer and your relationship with God as the primary source of healing. A homeopathic remedy is a God-given natural form of healing that works to break down the unhealthy emotional walls that hold you back from allowing God to get close enough to provide the healing you need. The longer you hold in emotions, the longer you will resist anyone to get emotionally close enough to help you change.

≈

STUDY QUESTIONS

1. How would this natural form of healing help with your situation?

2. What steps can you take to find a homeopathic experienced professional to assist with your treatment?

3. After reading this chapter, what additional insights have you learned about yourself and what can you do to change your life for the better?

Suggested Web sites for more information:

National Center for Homeopathy,
www.homeopathic.org

Homeopathic Educational Services,
www.homeopathic.com

North American Society of Homeopaths,
www.homeopathy.org

American Institute of Homeopathy,
www.homeopathyusa.org

American Association of Naturopathic
Physicians, www.naturopathic.org

15

STOP TRYING TO CHANGE YOUR UNEMOTIONAL MATE

~

When you look solely to your mate for satis-faction, disappointment awaits you.

If you have been living in an emotionless relationship for some time, you are probably more sad and discouraged than you realize. You may have become numb to your own feelings and lost your ability to gauge how you are supposed to emotionally react to people or situations. You may feel "blah," weighed down, or don't even know you have become emotionally dead inside. Maybe you are so disconnected from the relationship, you feel like you're on the very edge of a cliff, ready to fall off if something does not change. Like so many people, you may ask, "What can I do that I haven't already tried?" The answer is within your grasp! The following are ways to start making changes in your situation by changing how you live and respond to your circumstances.

Stop trying to receive from your mate what you are lacking in your own life.

Pam has always thought the lack of love and attention in her marriage could somehow be fixed if she would only work harder at making everything just right. When you are empty inside, it is common to believe if you work harder or if your spouse will change, then somehow you will be able to save the marriage, not be a failure, receive the love you never received, become good enough, or fix what is broken. Your own emptiness and fear of failing does not allow you to see that you are trying to fulfill your own needs from a person who cannot give you the very thing you want! Your dream to make your relationship work blinds you from seeing the miserable reality of living in an emotionless relationship. If you have not received it by now, you need to get the hint that your mate will not change because of what you have tried already. You need to stop exhausting yourself by trying to make everything perfect or by trying to fix your mate. Instead, look in the mirror and ask why you are so driven to make things right at the expense of your own needs and sanity.

Your drive to get love from your mate is often to fill the emptiness that was created when you did not receive love and attention from your early relationships. However, you should not try to "find" yourself, feel good about yourself, or fill an emotional emptiness through your mate. If this is what you expect, you will always struggle to get your needs met. You cannot fill an emotional emptiness created early in life from an unemotional adult that does not know how to show you the love you need! Looking to another person to supply your happiness is dangerous since that person will make mistakes and will say or do things that may hurt you. Instead, find healing for your own emptiness and then fill your heart with something greater than what you have known. This will be discussed in more detail in other chapters.

Stop trying to change someone that does not want to change.

More than anything, Pam wants to help her husband become the warm, loving mate she has always dreamed of having. However, the more she asks for hugs, kisses, or just talking together, the more frustrated and angry she becomes when he does not follow through on her requests. "Why do I have to ask my husband to show me love?" Pam asked me in frustration.

Isn't it odd that the very ways your unemotional mate hurts you and hurts the relationship are the very things he or she simply refuses to change? At the moment you want to knock some sense into your mate's head, is the very time he or she wants to argue and defend the behaviors that are making the relationship miserable. The more you try to tell your mate what to do, the more he or she may argue and dig their heels into the ground to avoid you or sabotage your efforts. Remember that your mate is living an unemotional life because of his or her own issues, and you can see those faults better than your mate can. Also remember, you are not the original reason for your mate being unemotional or miserable (even though they may blame you for it). However, knowing about those faults does not give you a license to bash them over your mate's head.

As much as you want your mate to change you need to stop trying to push your changes on your mate. The more you tell your mate what to do, the more he or she will not do what you ask! Instead, you need to focus on changing how you live your life and how you respond to your partner. You need to stop trying to change your mate to fulfill something in yourself and you need to stop trying to rescue your mate from something he or she does not yet realize they need. Rescue yourself from the bondage of trying to fulfill your dream through someone else. As you make changes, your mate will change because of how you react differently. This will be explained in later chapters.

Stop trying to rescue your mate

The more Pam sees how much Tony struggles with saying what he feels, socializing with others, or connecting with the children, the more she is always right behind him trying to make things work. Biblically, a wife should be supporting her husband by encouraging him and building him up. However, in emotionless relationships such as this, whenever Pam rescues Tony, it excuses him from taking on his adult responsibilities and sends the message that Tony does not need to try because Pam will do the work. For example, knowing Tony cannot express himself in front of others, Pam will speak for him on the telephone, during conversations, or make excuses why he does not participate with others.

Out of Pam's guilt, embarrassment, or feeling bad for the way Tony does not relate with others, Pam believes she must make excuses to friends and family (especially the children) to make up for his lack of involvement. Even though Pam believes she is helping Tony, her behaviors are actually making the situation worse. Pam would desperately like Tony to become more active with the kids and work together with decisions for the family. However, all the help Pam believes she is giving Tony is actually hindering him from growing spiritually, socially, and emotionally. With all the help he gets from Pam, Tony believes he does not need to take responsibility in doing his active part as a father, husband, or friend to others. Every time Pam makes an excuse to the children for Tony not being there, she is allowing him not to take responsibility for his duties as a father. Every time Pam speaks for Tony in front of others, whether it is on the telephone or in person, Tony is not being allowed to act his age and take responsibility for himself. Pam needs to tell Tony, "I believe it would be more appropriate that you answer the phone for yourself."

When Tony replies, "But I don't know what to say!" Pam needs to respond, "It would not be fair to you or to me if I spoke for you. Maybe it would be helpful if you went to counseling to learn how to express yourself."

Stop trying to make sense out of behaviors that do not make sense

When Tony becomes upset over a small issue, makes decisions that go against what Pam wants, has mood swings for no reason, or makes off the wall comments, Pam just shakes her head trying to figure out what is going on. Pam cannot count the number of days or nights she has spent trying to figure out why Tony acted irrational or made senseless comments. If you are spending your time and energy trying to figure out your mate, my best recommendation is to stop wasting your mental energy. You will not understand why the irrational or senseless behaviors occur because those actions are more child-like in nature and less understandable. Even your unemotional mate does not understand why the irrational behaviors happen, except when your mate blames you for what happens (which is probably most of the time).

To help you through this, remember this sentence: *When my mate does not make sense, I give myself permission not to make sense out of it.* The more you cannot figure out your mate, the less control you feel over your situation. As a result, you begin to feel helpless to do anything about what is happening. Helplessness can lead to other feelings such as depression and apathy. It's not worth losing your mind over so stop exhausting yourself with things that make no sense. Instead, put your energy into how you are reacting and finding ways to overcome your helplessness. You will learn more about this later in the book.

Setting boundaries

Setting boundaries is fundamental to letting others know how you think and feel about what you believe is important. To help you understand boundaries, here is an excerpt from my book, *When Feelings Don't Come Easy:*

Do you say 'Yes' when you really want to say "No?" Do you have a hard time letting people know what you need or feel? Do you allow yourself to be a doormat from rude comments or from being emotionally shut out? If the answer to these questions is, Yes, you have difficulty setting and respecting your own boundaries. When you respect yourself you are telling others what you believe is important and what you are willing to tolerate. You are setting your boundaries for what type of treatment you are willing to accept. If you allow insults, put-downs, time pressures, inappropriate comments, and unreasonable demands, you are allowing yourself to be disrespected. You need to verbalize your boundaries of respect and consideration to make others know where those boundaries begin and end. For example, if your husband, friend, or teenager is inappropriately yelling at you because they are angry, you have two choices. Either you can allow them to treat you like a doormat by allowing them to yell, or, you can let them know you want to be treated with respect by setting your boundaries. You can say, "You can tell me you are angry, but I do not appreciate you yelling at me. If you do that again I will leave the room until you can speak more calmly." You must take responsibility for setting boundaries with others. You have every right to expect people to take responsibility for their own actions. If they are an adult (or teenager) and do not take responsibility for their own actions, you should not have to put up with their irresponsibility. You have every right to expect the other person to treat you with respectful words and actions.

Not allowing yourself to express your own thoughts and feelings will make it difficult to set adequate boundaries in your life. When someone speaks rudely and you feel hurt, in order to set your boundaries it is important to express your feelings of hurt and dislike of their tone of voice. If you are hurt by someone and choose not to do anything about that hurt, you are giving the message, I allow you to disrespect me and treat me like a doormat.[28]

You must take responsibility for setting boundaries at home, work, school, and even church, otherwise you will have no one else to blame except yourself for how the other person treats you. You have every right to expect people to take responsibility for their own actions and you should not have to live with their irresponsibility. You have every right to expect the other person to treat you with respectful words and actions.

Beware of how you are treated

The harder you try to forcefully change another person who has been hurtful to you, the more that person may hurt back. If someone is still hurting you, here are some suggestions:

1. Do not put yourself in a position to get hurt. Keep your emotional and/or physical distance from hurtful people (this will be harder with your mate) until you become more confident with saying your feelings. If you are asked why you are distancing yourself, say, "I am making some changes in my life and need time to figure things out." Do not give details that can be used against you later.

2. Once you become more confident in yourself, express your feelings to the person who hurts you. For example, you may say, "It hurts me when you say that. I am asking you not to say that to me anymore." If the other person responds with more hurtful statements, realize they are not ready for your feelings. If you cannot say how you feel, journal your feelings or talk to a friend or a counselor.

DOMESTIC VIOLENCE

In your quest to improve or fix a relationship, you may become blind to how you are being treated emotionally, physically, sexually, and economically. From your own desire to make things work, it is important that you not allow your mate, boss, parents, friend, etc., to take advantage of you through methods of power and control. You may not realize that how people treat you can be considered domestic violence. It may be hard for you to see domestic violence happening in your own home and mistakenly believe it is only limited to physical abuse. Domestic violence exists in the following forms:

Emotional abuse: Criticisms, silent treatment, name-calling, belittling, hurtful statements, mind games, using the past against you, openly telling others about personal matters.

Intimidation: Instilling fear or control by using comments, actions, gestures, body language, a loud voice, throwing things, or destroying property.

Sexual abuse: Having sex against your will, treating you like a sex object, belittling or criticisms when you do not want sex.

Threats/Emotional blackmail: Verbalizing or carrying out threats to get what they want or making threatening statements toward you or a family member.

Physical abuse: Twisting arms, pushing, hitting, slapping, choking, pulling hair, or kicking.

Economic abuse: Keeping you from obtaining or quitting a job, controlling money, giving an "allowance," or limiting access to bank accounts.

Using superior attitude: Treating you like a servant, not involving you in family decisions, acting like the "master of the castle," or lording authority over you.

Religious abuse: Using God or scripture as a means to get you to do something against your will or as a form of judgment, punishment or criticism. Statements like, "And you call yourself a Christian," "God will get you for that," "God is not pleased with you," or "You're going to hell."

If there is domestic violence in your life, seek help to learn how to change your situation as soon as possible. You do not deserve this treatment and God does not want you to be subjected it. You do have a choice whether to put up with this.

If you do not feel safe, it will be harder to change yourself

You can read all the books about healing, go to the greatest counselor, and pray night and day, but until you feel physically and emotionally safe where you live, you may feel too uncomfortable (or afraid) to start making changes. For example, if your mate has a history of being critical, emotionally unsupportive, or physically hurtful, you would not feel safe to cry or say what you feel in front of your mate. You would be too afraid those feelings would be used against you. If you do not feel comfortable expressing your feelings or standing up for what you believe with the significant people in your life, seek counseling to learn what you can do about the situation.

WORDS OF ENCOURAGEMENT

Are you living for your mate? Are you trying to rescue your relationship? Do you feel safe to express your thoughts and feelings? You will not find the answers in your relationship, no matter how hard you try to fix it. No matter where you are in the relationship, evaluate what and whom you are living for. You need to find your faith in someone greater than your mate.

Personal Reflection

Lord, strengthen my heart with your mighty power. Great are you Lord to give me control and understanding in this relationship. Lord sustain me through my difficult times and cast

out the wickedness that will interfere with what you want
in this relationship. (Psalms 147:5,6 Paraphrased)

≈

STUDY QUESTIONS

1. What are you trying to receive from your mate that you are lacking in your own life?

2. How are you trying to change your mate?

3. What can you do differently to decrease your dependency or desire to change your mate?

4. What does your mate do that does not make sense and what can you do differently to change how you react to that?

5. Do you need to set boundaries in your relationships? If yes, make a list of those boundaries.

6. Describe any domestic violence that may be happening in your relationship and what you will do about it.

7. Why is it harder to change when you do not feel safe? Explain if this is happening.

8. Explain who are you living for—your mate, yourself, or God?

9. After reading this chapter, what additional insights have you learned about yourself and what can you do to change your life for the better?

16

THE EMOTIONAL MATE CAN
MAKE HEALTHY CHANGES

~

*Finding worth and happiness through other
people only makes you dependent on them.*

Pam spoke with tears in her eyes as she shared about her loneliness and hurt throughout her marriage with Joe. Pam realized she had spent most of the marriage trying to fix Joe into the warm, loving mate she had always dreamt of having. After many years, the more Pam did not receive love, the more she would bury herself in other relationships or activities to satisfy her emptiness. Over time, the lack of love and attention from Joe created sadness that grew heavier each year. Pam began to resent what was happening and did not want to live this way any more. Yet she felt trapped and helpless to do anything about it.

If you have been living in a relationship like Pam, you probably have accumulated your own large amount of emotional hurts. The longer you allow these negative emotions to remain inside, the greater potential for feeling stressed out, helpless, and emotionally numb. Elizabeth Somer, in her book, *Food and Mood* emphasizes that the accumulated stress of your circumstances can take a toll on your health. She quotes "Robert Russell, M.D., professor of medicine and nutrition at Tufts University who warns that, 'The effects of stress on health and aging may be greater than we think . . . ' In fact, stress is a major player in mood, food cravings, thinking, insomnia, and all aspects of emotional and physical health."[29] Those words of warning are important to remember as you learn to change how you live and respond to your situation.

HEAL YOUR UNHEALTHY EMOTIONS

If you are struggling with feelings of hurt, helplessness, sadness, being trapped, or emotional numbness, you must begin to realize these are your feelings and you are the only person responsible for them. In order to change how you feel you must give yourself enough space from the situation (and spouse) to grow emotionally, physically, and spiritually. This will enable you to heal and respond in a healthy way. Here are some steps to take:

How to heal and grow emotionally:

1. Give yourself permission to express your feelings regardless of your situation. It is very important that you begin identifying and expressing your emotions as soon as you can when something happens to you. For example, let's say your mate makes a rude comment and you cannot say anything about your hurt because your comments will only make your situation worse. Begin identifying and expressing your hurt feelings in a journal, to a friend, or to God in prayer. You can say or write out your feelings when you ask yourself: *What am I feeling inside? Why do I feel this way? What am I going to do with these feelings?* This is discussed in more detail in the chapter, "How to Communicate Your Feelings."

2. Identify, let go, and heal the hurt emotions you have from your current and past relationships. Any old rejection, resentment, or unforgiveness from the past will act as a heavy

weight on your heart and mind. This will only increase the depression and sadness in your life. To stop letting your situation control your emotions use these steps:

a. Find a quiet and uninterrupted time where you can privately think about your current relationship and the important relationships in your past.

b. Starting with your current relationship, write what it has been like to live in each relationship:

- List the way you have been treated (verbally, physically, emotionally, sexually, and emotionally, etc.) Describe what happened using as much detail as possible and identify the feelings with each hurtful situation.

- Identify as many feelings as you can that go along with how you have been treated. To help you identify feelings, you will find a feelings chart in the appendix.

- Read your feelings to a trusted friend, counselor, or pray aloud to God.

c. You can let go by praying this prayer with each hurt you identify: "God, forgive me for holding on to the spirit of (name the negative emotion). God, have your Son, Jesus, release me from the spirit of (name the negative emotion). God, replace this negative spirit with the spirit of (name the opposite positive emotion). I ask this in the name of Jesus Christ."

3. Do not allow yourself to go through this alone; find a friend (of the same gender) to call whenever you need someone with whom to talk.

4. You may benefit from my first book, *When Feelings Don't Come Easy.*

How to heal and grow physically:

1. Begin to separate your physical needs from the needs of your mate. If you are not treated with love and respect, then you need to stop begging, nagging, and pleading for your mate to give you what your mate cannot give at this point. Here are some examples:

   a. It's 10:00 p.m. and you want to go to bed because you are very tired. However, your husband (who frequently stays up late) insists you stay up with him to watch television. You can say, "Honey, I would like to do that, but I am very tired and I really need to go to bed." Your husband responds by arguing, "You're always tired. You never want to do anything with me." At this point, anything you say to justify going to bed will not make your selfish mate understand why you need rest. Do not argue with your mate since he probably is only focused on his own needs. Calmly say, "I would appreciate it if you would consider my needs. We can spend time together tomorrow night." Take care of yourself and go to bed.

   b. If you want your mate to stop making rude comments during a conversation, you have two choices. Either tell your mate you don't appreciate the comments or you can leave the room to separate yourself from what is happening. You do not deserve to be treated with disrespect by your mate (or children, parents, friends, etc.) at anytime.

   c. Let's say you haven't gone out to dinner for some time and you ask your mate to go out. If your mate does not want to go (and there is no reason he or she should refuse), you may say, "We don't go out very often and I would really like to go out together. If you don't want to go, I will ask a friend." If your mate still does not want to go out, call a friend (of the same gender) and have a good time!

2. Take better care of yourself. No matter how you are cared for by your mate, start caring for yourself. It is not a sin to love and respect yourself. Allow yourself to have fun and enjoy life with other positive thinking friends. Pamper yourself. You deserve to be treated nicely. Do something you enjoy at least once a week. When was the last time you felt special or did something fun? There will be more information about this later in the book.

3. Seek Christian counseling to learn more about what you can do for yourself and for your situation.

How to heal and grow spiritually:

Do not allow yourself to go through this alone; involve people you trust and ask them to pray for you and with you. It is extremely important that you find prayer partners to pray specifically for your situation. If it has been difficult to pray or you have given up on God, remember that God has not given up on you. He wants you to learn more about yourself through this situation. "The Lord is close to the brokenhearted and saves those who are crushed in spirit. A righteous man may have many troubles, but the Lord delivers him from them all," (Psalms 34:18,19). Pray specifically for your situation. See the chapter "Finding Strength Through Prayer" for more details.

YOU CAN CHANGE YOUR SITUATION

I could see the frustration in Pam's face as she described all the activities she organized for the family. Pam admitted to being resentful that Joe was not doing more with the family, and she felt powerless in knowing how to get him to help more. Pam could not believe it when I told her that Joe's expectation for her to do so much was because of his own helplessness and dependence on her. I reassured her that she actually had more control and influence over Joe than she realized. Let me explain.

Similar to Pam, you may be frustrated with how much work you must do around the home or how much you must do to keep the communication, love, and affection going in the relationship. Since your unemotional mate does not have much experience in having a loving relationship, he or she is dependent on you to keep the relationship and family stabilized. As difficult as it may be to believe this, your mate is very dependent on you and could not survive in the relationship (or family) without you. In other words, you actually have more influence to change the relationship than you believe.

For example, if you have been working hard to maintain the relationship (encouraging communication, emotions, attention, affection, etc.), your mate has become more dependent on you than you may realize. Since your mate does not relate to people, you are the most important relationship he or she has in life (but your mate does not understand that). Without your work and encouragement, the relationship would fall apart. If you stopped trying to fix your mate or left the relationship, your mate would lose everything. I am not advocating you leave the relationship; instead, I am emphasizing how much influence you have to make a significant change in the relationship. This is why it is so important for you to stand up for what is respectful, what you believe, and what you need. Because your mate is so dependent on you, he or she will change when you make changes.

Pam listed all the household chores and activities that she had to constantly remind Joe to help with. "I'm tired of reminding Joe and telling him what to do. I want him to act like my husband and not act like one of the children," Pam said in frustration. I told Pam this was often a common problem in emotionless homes where the emotional mate will overcompensate for what the unemotional mate does not do. Over the years, to make the relationship work, Pam began taking on more of the responsibilities around the house and acted as Joe's personal secretary, reminding him what to do next. Unfortunately, each time Pam tried to remind Joe, it became a battle because he resented being told what to do. Pam felt like she was in a no-win situation.

In Pam's quest to make the relationship work, she had become more like a mother than a wife. Whether it was from her need to please others, fear that Joe would get upset, or the need to make everything right, Pam took on more of the responsibilities. Unfortunately, this sent a message that Pam would always be available to do the work and enabled Joe to not to take his responsibilities seriously. Through counseling, Pam realized she needed to step back and change her own behavior and increase her expectations for Joe. Pam had to learn why she needed to "rescue" Joe and learn how to respond differently to his irresponsibility.

You should have the right to stand up for what you need, feel, and believe. You must choose to take the first step to find the power and influence that is available through God, friends, professionals, and especially the capabilities within yourself. If you do not choose those resources, you are choosing not to grow and allowing your mate to take advantage of you. The best way to change your situation is to change how you handle your circumstances. When you change how you think, feel, and respond to your situation, your mate will have no choice but to respond differently. More details about how you can change are explained later in the book.

WHEN YOUR WORTH IS IN QUESTION

After all the years of trying to make the relationship better, Pam started crying when she admitted she felt like a failure. "I've tried to get Joe to talk to me for so long, I stopped trying. I guess it is not meant to be." When you are not able to freely express your thoughts and feelings, you lose your own self worth and identity. Over time, you settle to live this way because you do not believe you are worthy or deserve to receive anything better. As a result, you become stuck in a situation where you believe (or feel) that you are helpless to change it, and you resign yourself to living that way. My question to you is why are you settling to live that way? Why are you settling for less love and respect than you deserve?

A major reason why you allow yourself to live this way is because you doubt your own self-worth! How people have treated you throughout your life has created a negative message (or belief) that you are not worthy of respect. The years of emotionless living have only made this belief stronger. If you don't believe this, then why are you settling to live in a relationship where you do not receive the love you want and deserve? Why are you accepting disrespect from your mate when he or she does not encourage emotions? Why are you allowing yourself to feel alone and unhappy? Would you treat your best friend the way your unemotional mate treats you? Would you ignore your best friend and allow them to emotionally suffer without trying to do something for them? Of course you wouldn't; you would want something much better for them. Then why are you allowing yourself to be treated this way? You're worth more than that! When your self-worth is low, it becomes hard to say what you feel or stand up for what you believe in. You put others first, at the expense of your own wellbeing, and you believe you must work harder for the right to earn respect and happiness. These are all deceptions that have kept you from realizing you are worthy and deserve to be treated with respect and love. As long as you allow the relationship to stay the same, you are sending a message to your mate that the relationship is fine and he or she can ignore what you feel, think, and believe. As long as you let your mate treat you this way, you are allowing your mate to disrespect you. Your life is far more worthy than what *you* have been settling for.

FIND YOUR WORTHINESS

I know how worthy you are because God made you worthy and the Bible is very clear about it. "For we are God's workmanship, created in Christ Jesus to do good works, which God prepared in advance for us to do" (Ephesians 2:10). This means you deserve to be loved, honored, and respected, especially from your mate. It is very healthy to want the fulfillment of love, appreciation, and acceptance from your mate. However, as long as you solely look to your mate for the fulfillment of security, happiness, and love, you are destined for disappointment. Even if your mate suddenly changed into everything you ever dreamed, you would not have the fulfillment you seek. If you believe you are not complete or worthy without your mate, you may fall into the category of being codependent. Codependency is a dependence, clinging, and/or control of others to satisfy your own fear of not getting your own needs met without that relationship. Unemotional people are too selfish and unpredictable to even attempt to satisfy your needs. You cannot find your worthiness or happiness solely from another person who may disappoint you. The God that created you also wants a relationship with you and wants to help you. "God is able to make all grace abound to you, so that in all things at all times, having all that you need, you will abound in every good work," (2 Corinthians 9:8). You will learn more about this in the chapter

"Finding Strength Through Prayer." To remind yourself how worthy you are, write down the following list on small cards. Place the cards around your house and place of work. Say these positive statements everyday.

- I am good enough.
- I am precious in God's sight.
- God loves me and forgives me.
- I am a unique and wonderful person.
- I am free to express the feelings that God gave me.
- I do not need to listen to or believe the destructive mesages I hear today.
- I can accept the good things that happen today.

SUMMARY

1. The longer you try to directly change your mate, the more you will feel disappointed. The longer you blame your mate for not giving you what you want, the longer you will feel miserable. You have the choice to be different.

2. Recognize you cannot directly change your mate—give that headache to God. Seek counseling to help you work through your situation.

3. Focus your energy on something greater than your mate; focus on who you are in God.

4. When you change how you think, feel, and respond to your situation, your mate will have no choice but to respond differently. You have more influence to change your situation than you believe.

5. To feel good about yourself, find a way to use your own

abilities, talents, and desires in a creative way. You have the choice to feel good about yourself.

6. Give yourself permission to find help if you are in an abusive relationship.

7. You have the choice to identify and express the emotions God created within you.

8. You have the choice to seek counseling to help you sort out your feelings and situation.

TAKE CARE OF YOURSELF

For those of you living in an emotionless relationship, you must get out from under the emotional oppression that weighs you down, clouding your view of reality, and hindering you from functioning at your best. As you start feeling better about yourself and stand up against your mate's disrespect, your mate will do all they can to keep you from changing. If your mate becomes more disrespectful when you stand up against his or her comments, stand firm, knowing that you deserve love and respect. Find strength through prayer, friends, and professional help. Whether you want to believe it or not, you have a choice whether to change yourself and your relationship. However, radical steps on your part will need to be taken and you have the power to choose what to do (this will be explained in more detail in later chapters). If you are experiencing symptoms of constant unhappiness, poor motivation, struggling to do your daily routine, frequent crying, strong feelings to get out of the relationship, I recommend you seek counseling. For more information, see the appendix regarding how to find a counselor. Remember, "My flesh and my heart may fail, but God is the strength of my heart and my portion forever," (Psalms 73:26).

Personal Reflection

God, help me to see the things
that are getting in the way of finding joy in life
and help me to know how worthy you have made me.

≈

STUDY QUESTIONS

1. What emotional baggage do you have in your own life?

2. How can you grow emotionally, physically, and spiritually?

3. What influence do you have to change yourself and your situation?

4. Do you feel worthy and deserving of love and respect? If not, how can you improve your own self-worth?

5. After reading this chapter, what additional insights have you learned about yourself and what can you do to change your life for the better?

17

FINDING STRENGTH THROUGH PRAYER

~

*"Therefore, I tell you, whatever you ask for in prayer,
believe that you have received it, and it will be yours,"*
(Mark 11:24)
We have to pray with our eyes on God, not on the difficulties.
—Oswald Chambers

According to the Center for the Study of Religion/ Spirituality and Health at Duke University Medical Center, personal faith, praying, Bible reading, and being involved in a church has shown to be among the strongest ways to bring hope in any struggling circumstance. For twenty-five years the Duke Center has conducted over twenty-five research studies that have found that people who pray regularly and have religion as an important part of their lives, "often experience less depression, less anxiety, greater hope, more purpose and meaning, and recover more quickly from health-damaging emotions such as depression. It is during the most stressful times and difficult circumstances that religion often separates those who are able to cope from those who are not. Often, it is the suffering itself that drives people to God, that motivates them to develop spiritually, that makes them realize that they cannot by themselves cope with their problems. However, having a deep religious faith does equip people with a powerful tool to help them endure and conquer their problems."[30] You do have the choice to use prayer as a means to find hope and change how you feel, think, and react to your situation. Even if you have been praying for some time but feel like your prayers have not been answered, the power of prayer is still working.

Regardless of how your prayers have turned out, God still is in the business of healing and the Bible still promises that "God will meet all your needs according to his glorious riches in Jesus Christ," (Philippians 4:19). In the workbook called, Experiencing God, authors Henry Blackaby and Claude King emphasize that God is telling you, "I want you to love me above everything else. When you are in a relationship of love with Me, you have everything there is. To be loved by God is the highest relationship, the highest achievement, and the highest position in life."[31]

The important message to learn from this chapter is that God is always with you no matter what your situation and you need to focus on how God can work in you and for you. If your energy and attention is focused on changing someone else then you will be blinded to see what God has for you. You will be so busy fretting about the other person you will miss everything God wants to give you and ultimately miss getting what you really need to change your situation. The way to change your situation is to first focus your attention on your relationship with God to see what He has in store for you. Secondly, pray for your situation by focusing on how God can change your own understanding, attitude, and approach toward whatever you are facing. Ask God to work through your circumstances, people, prayer, and the Bible. As you read this chapter, ask God to open your heart and mind to how you can use the information to change your life.

FINDING GOD FOR THE FIRST TIME

God is real. He came to earth as Jesus Christ and He

wants to be your personal friend, comforter, helper, Savior, protector, and Heavenly Father. Prayer is how to have a two way conversation with God. Don't be afraid to pour out your complaints, hurts, anger, desires, and needs. God has very big shoulders and can take whatever you dish out. He wants you to ask for everything and He wants you to be specific about your needs. By asking specifically, it forces you to focus more on what you need and helps you become intentional with your requests. Start having a daily conversation with God as a personal friend, either in your thoughts, talking aloud, or writing to Him in a journal.

If you expect God to answer your prayers in a powerful way, you need to establish a relationship with Him. Knowing Jesus in your heart will provide you with the most effective and powerful strength to combat the battle you are facing. Realize that anyone who accepts Jesus becomes a new person with God. "Therefore, if anyone is in Christ, he is a new creation; the old has gone, the new has come," (2 Corinthians 5:17). Jesus is waiting for you to accept Him into your life as your personal Savior and friend. "That if you confess with your mouth, 'Jesus is Lord,' and believe in your heart that God raised him from the dead, you will be saved," (Romans 10:9). If you would like to have a personal relationship with Jesus Christ say these words to God in prayer: *"Dear God, I realize I am lost without you and I need you to help me find my way. Please come into my heart as my Lord and Savior to guide my life. In the name of Jesus Christ I pray."* Write down the date you prayed and let someone close to you know about your decision.

REVITALIZE YOUR RELATIONSHIP WITH GOD

Living an emotionless life is like walking in the desert. Even if you have had a relationship with God for some time, your spiritual life can become as dry as a bone, feeling as if your prayers have gone unheard for years. For those of you that need to be spiritually restored remember, "And the God of all grace, who called you to his eternal glory in Christ, after you have suffered a little while, will himself restore you and make you strong, firm and steadfast. To him be the power for ever and ever," (1 Peter 5:10–11). Take time, right now, and recommit your life and situation over to Jesus Christ by praying, "*Dear Lord, I have fallen away and not trusted in you; please forgive me. Help me to recommit my heart, mind, and soul to you. Show me the way, in the name of Jesus Christ.*" Write down the date you prayed.

EARTHLY FATHER, HEAVENLY FATHER

One important influence on your ability to have a relationship with God is the type of relationships you had with authority figures as a child (especially your father). Eric prays and attends church with his family, but has always struggled with his relationship with God. He never could understand how people could "hear from God" or "feel close" to God. When I asked Eric about is parents, he said his father worked long hours and did not have much time to play with him. Eric remembered how angry his mother would become when his father stayed out late or broke a promise. Eric had a hard time talking to his father and had a hard time trusting his word. Like Eric, the connection between what you experienced from your earthly father has everything to do with your ability to get emotionally close to your Heavenly Father. If your father was emotionally and physically unavailable, chances are you would have difficulty believing your Heavenly Father cares what is on your heart or wants to hear your prayers. If you believed you did not measure up to the expectations of your caregivers, you may find it difficult to measure up to what God expects of you. If your caregivers used threats or punishment to keep you in line as a child, you may have a similar fear of what God will do if you do something wrong.

You may say, "God is not my earthly father, why would I act the same toward God?"

If you did not learn anything different, how you love, trust, experience fear, and express yourself will be the same with God as it was with your parents. If you were not told or learned any other way, why would you know how to relate to God any differently? It is important that you begin to separate the unavailable, fallible authority figures of your childhood from the compassionate, loving, infallible Heavenly Father. If you need to change how you relate with God, you may benefit from counseling with a pastor or Christian therapist.

EXPECTING GOD TO WORK IN YOUR LIFE

God handles your requests by answering with YES, NO, or WAIT. Think about it. The same is true with someone you care about. For example, when you are asked for something by a young child, you would allow that child to receive what they want depending on his or her maturity and ability. You may say, "yes," if they are ready to handle it; "no," if they cannot handle it, or "wait," if they need to grow more before they can handle it. The same is true with your relationship with God. If your prayers have not been answered the way you want, chances are God has something else in mind for you. Prayer is a direct link with God. However, most people only use prayer as a means to *tell* God what they want and what they think should happen. However, your desires may be different from God's desires for your life at that time. In your own life, how often would you give your young children everything they asked for? How often have your children cried, questioned your loyalty, become sad, or become angry, all because you did not give them what they wanted, when they wanted?

The same goes for your relationship with your Heavenly Father. He knows what you need far better than you know. However, when you do not get what you *want* or get it *your way,* do you become disappointed and believe God is against you? Did you know your Heavenly Father wants you to find happiness, just like you want to have happiness for the people you love? If you are not getting what you want right now, it is not because God is mad at you, punishing you, not listening to you, or thinks you are a bad person. Instead, your Heavenly Father has a better plan for you, just like you have better plans for your children. "For I know the plans I have for you,' declares the LORD, 'plans to prosper you and not to harm you, plans to give you hope and a future," (Jeremiah 29:11). Just like a wise parent, God knows what is best for you and when you are ready to receive it.

INCREASE YOUR PRAYER POWER

Prayer by itself is one of the most powerful, effective, and available sources of help to make things happen, especially for circumstances that you have no control over. A study was done in 2000 at St. Luke's Hospital in Kansas City, Missouri, where doctors looked at 990 patients who had been admitted to a cardiac-unit. The study showed that half of the group that were prayed for by an outside group for one month showed fewer complications than those patients not prayed for. The only conclusion that the University of Missouri in Kansas City, who headed the study could suggest was, "an association exists between being prayed for and having an improved outcome."[32]

Prayer coverage increases the power and authority of the Holy Spirit, binds the enemy, and pleases the Lord. "The Lord is near to all who call on him, to all who call on him in truth," (Psalm 145:18). For example, find prayer partners, such as friends, family, and church members to pray about your situation. Keep them informed on a regular basis how to pray for you. "Therefore confess your sins to each other and pray for each other so that you may be healed. The prayer of a righteous man is powerful and effective," (James 5:16).

LOOKING FOR ANSWERS TO PRAYER

The reason why you do not know what God is doing for you may be that you do not know how to look for what God is doing. God is ALWAYS pursuing a relationship with you and God is ALWAYS working in your life. "Jesus said to them, My Father is always at work to this day, and I, too, am working," (John 5:17).

It is hard to see what God is doing when you are focused on only what you want and consumed with your own circumstances. If you are consumed with changing your mate and that is not happening, God has something else in mind. God's first desire is for you to come into a loving relationship with Him. When you have a relationship with God, you will know Him better and you will be better able to understand what He desires for your life. You will find joy in life through that relationship. "If you obey my commands, you will remain in my love, just as I have obeyed my Father's commands and remain in his love. I have told you this so that my joy may be in you and that your joy may be complete," (John 15:10–11). Seeing God work in your life can be very difficult for people living in an emotionless life. This is primarily due to the difficulty in getting close to people in relationships. God primarily speaks to you by the Holy Spirit through the Bible, prayer, circumstances, and people.

CIRCUMSTANCES AND PEOPLE:

When you pray, watch how God works in your life. Since God wants the best for you, He may give you something different than what you originally asked. Do not sit and wait for what you ask for. Instead, consider whatever happens in front of you as God working toward the eventual goal of bringing you into a closer relationship with Him and you getting what you need. Even though you are not going to always understand why things happen, you can decide what to do with what happens. You have a choice: *you can either see circumstances as a problem that are obstructing your life, or you can use circumstances as an opportunity to learn what you need to do differently.*

PRAYER:

Prayer is as much about hearing from God as it is about you telling God what you want. Prayer is a way for God to tell you what He wants of you. "This is the confidence we have in approaching God: that if we ask anything according to his will, he hears us. And if we know that he hears us - whatever we ask- we know that we have what we asked of him," (1 John 5:14–15).

BIBLE:

The Word of God is also a powerful way for God to tell you what He wants of you. "All Scripture is God-breathed and is useful for teaching, rebuking, correcting and training in righteousness, so that the man of God may be thoroughly equipped for every good work," (2 Timothy 3:16–17). Find time to read the Bible. Before you read, pray for God to give you understanding of His Word. Start reading in the New Testament and meditate on what you read.

ENCOURAGING THE FAITH OF YOUR MATE

The first rule is not to push God on others. Rather exemplify what God would want you to show through your attitude, faith, and the peace that Christ has accomplished in your life. You must focus on changing yourself into what God wants you to be and not try to change your mate into what you think they need to be. If you are trying to act like a Christian to impress your mate rather than living the life of a Christian, you will fail. Your mate will detect what you are doing, use it against you, and you will not be able to last through the next argument. Don't be tempted to get on the treadmill of trying to defend every little thing your mate says or does against you. When you focus on changing yourself first, your mate will also start to change.

LET GOD DO THE CHANGING

Helping your unemotional mate find a relationship with Christ is really about you letting go and letting God do the changing. You need to change by getting out of the way. When you pray for God to change you to be the best person God wants you to be, you are actually making changes in a powerful way. If you pray for your mate, he or she will make changes. However, the changes may not be what you expect or in the time frame you would like. Let God take care of your mate so you can stay focused on your relationship with God and make the necessary changes within yourself. He will provide what you need, "And my God will meet all your needs according to His glorious riches in Christ Jesus," (Philippians 4:19). Keep praying for opportunities to provide encouraging words about how Christ is working in your life. Use statements like, "Wow, it was really beyond coincidence today when that person helped me." Telling your mate how much he or she needs God will only annoy your mate. I strongly recommend you pray specifically and regularly for:

1. God to take away any attitude of anger, hostility, resentment, judgment that you may have toward your mate. "Get rid of all bitterness, rage and anger, brawling and slander, along with every form of malice. Be kind and compassionate to one another, forgiving each other, just as in Christ God forgave you," (Ephesians 4:31, 32).

2. An attitude of openness for God to work in your heart.

3. God's wisdom for the right words of encouragement and opportunities for you to share about Christ.

4. God to work through people and circumstances in your mate's life to witness in ways that you cannot. "I can do everything through Him who gives me strength," (Philippians 4:13).

5. God to bring healing of the heart, mind, and soul either through the direct work of God or through a professional.

6. Allow God's Word to change your life, by incorporating God's Word into your daily prayers and meditate on the powerful Word of God. Start praying right now. Write down the following prayer on a card, say it each day, and meditate on the message throughout the day. Allow God's word to change your life! Pray this prayer regularly, *Dear Lord, give me a new heart and put a new spirit in me; remove my heart of stone and give me a heart of flesh* (Ezekiel 36:26 paraphrased).

WORDS OF ENCOURAGEMENT:

You don't have to feel like you're knocking your head against the wall, trying to change your situation. Allow God to help you by putting Him on your team. Whether you "feel" His presence or not, God promises to be with you when you pray. Stand on the promises of God! Allow God's Word to change your life starting today! Incorporate God into your life by praying to Him in everything you do and watch Him work before you.

Personal Reflection

Write down the following prayer on a card, say it each day, and meditate on the message throughout the day:

Dear Lord, give me a new heart and put a new spirit in me; remove my heart of stone and give me a heart of flesh, (Ezekiel 36:26 paraphrased).

STUDY QUESTIONS

1. Describe where you are in your faith walk with God and how you know or do not know God personally.

2. Describe how you can change how you pray.

3. Describe how you can change how you expect God to work in your life.

4. Describe how you can change how you expect God to answer prayer.

5. Describe how you can change your relationship with God.

6. After reading this chapter, what additional insights have you learned about yourself and what can you do to change your relationship with God for the better?

18

HOW TO COMMUNICATE YOUR FEELINGS

~

If facts are the seeds that later produce knowledge and wisdom, then the emotions and the impressions of the senses are the fertile soil, which the seeds must grow.
—Rachel Carson

A little girl is setting up house with small chairs around a table. As she carefully put the cups, dishes, spoons, and forks at each table setting, she talked aloud to her imaginary friends. "Now put the cups right here so Billy Bear can reach it and the forks go right next to the plate for Dolly." You can hear the delight in her voice as she enjoys every minute of her playtime. Her voice changes as she gives detailed instructions to each stuffed friend. The noise from her brother playing on the other side of the room starts to get louder. Without warning her brother comes closer making the annoying sound, "Vrrroooom," that she tries to ignore. Her pesky brother waves his jet through the air with a flight plan that is heading straight for the table. He dive-bombs Billy Bear's perfectly placed plate and cup: "Vrrroooom - kerboooom" the little boy bellows as he knocks over the bear. Suddenly there is an ear-piercing shriek from the little girl. "Eeeeekk, get away, get away; you're hurting Billy Bear." The jet pilot comes up from the dive bombing mission and goes into emergency procedures to escape the enemy, "Vrrroooom," comes from the boy as the jet heads home from a mission accomplished.

Males have uttered noises and females have communicated emotions since early childhood. How many of you hear grown men mumbling similar noises and grown women voicing similar complaints just like this little boy and girl. Ironically, for many of us the communication patterns have not changed much over the years; we just get older. Growing up in an emotionless home where you do not learn to express emotions only makes the difference between men and women worse. The good news is that it's never too late to learn how to communicate your emotions to one another. You might as well start now.

SAYING WHAT YOU FEEL

The key to changing old ways of the past is to learn new ways to respond. One way to develop appropriate patterns of expression is to release what you feel either at the time the event happens or sometime soon after. When you let out your feelings, you will be less overwhelmed and reduce the need for emotional outbursts. When you are emotionally or physically hurt, God intended tears to be released. The more you let out the hurt, the faster you will heal. According to Bernie S. Siegel, MD, in his book, *Peace, Love and Healing*, he emphasizes "It's important to express all your feelings, including the unpleasant ones, because once they're out they lose their power over you; they can't tie you up in knots anymore. Letting them out is a call for help and a 'live' message to your body."[33]

Even the Bible tells of people expressing anger, sadness, fear, jealousy, sorrow, joy, etc. The wisdom of the Bible informs you that feelings are allowed and that you must have control over how you express them. These emotions are given as a natural function to release energy and communicate with others. If you do not use these sources of expression in your daily life, you will not experience life to its fullest potential. If you want to release the emotions you feel inside, you must give yourself permission to constructively release your feelings.

EXAMPLES OF EXPRESSING EMOTIONS

It can be a struggle to express emotions if that is something you have not learned to do. One of the best examples of expressing emotions comes from the life of Jesus Christ found in the Bible. Actually, God desires that everyone seeks a relationship with Jesus to follow His examples. Philippians 4:9 states, "Whatever you have learned or received or heard from me, or seen in me - put it into practice. And the God of peace will be with you." Here are some examples that illustrate how Jesus expressed feelings.

Tears

Jesus went to the place where His good friend Lazarus was buried. The Bible states that when Jesus looked around at the people crying over Lazarus's death, "Jesus wept" with compassion (John 11:35).

Anger

During the Jewish Holy time of year called Passover, it was the custom of the people to sacrifice an unblemished animal in order to receive forgiveness of their sins. The temple courtyard became an open marketplace. "So he [Jesus] made a whip out of cords, and drove all from the temple area, both sheep and cattle; he scattered the coins of the money changers and overturned their tables. To those who sold doves he said, "Get these out of here! How dare you turn my Father's house into a market," (John 2:16). During this situation Jesus revealed

His *frustration,* and showed a rare but clear expression of *anger* toward those who were making a mockery of the temple.

Fear and agony

In the Garden of Gethsemane, moments before His arrest by the Romans, Jesus prayed alone to God. "Father, if you are willing, take this cup from me; yet not my will, but yours be done . . . And being in anguish, he prayed more earnestly, and his sweat was like drops of blood falling to the ground," (Luke 22:42, 44). As a physician, the apostle Luke was able to describe the rare phenomenon called, *hemathidrosis,* where a person will sweat blood under tremendous *emotional stress, fear, or agony.* The human side of Jesus showed through His physical and emotional reactions.

Rejection and sadness

During the sentencing of Jesus, the Roman Governor, Pilate, asked the crowd of Jews what they wanted to do with Jesus. Their reply was "Take him away! Take him away! Crucify him! We have no king but 'Caesar," (John 19:15). That would be a tremendous time of *sadness* and *rejection* when His own people shouted to have Jesus taken away to be killed through crucifixion.

Joy

Jesus repeatedly tried to reassure the disciples that He would return after He went away. Toward the end of His ministry, the disciples finally understood what Jesus was saying. Jesus *joyfully* remarked to the disciples, "You believe at last, Jesus answered,"(John 16:31).

The Bible clearly tells you to, "Be imitators of God," (Ephesians 5:1), and God gave you Jesus as the example to imitate. As the Divine Son of God and the earthly son of Joseph, Jesus Christ had the ability to experience all human emotions while living on the earth. If you want the best human example and you want to live like Jesus Christ in your heart, mind, and actions, then you should identify and express your feelings as portrayed by Jesus. If God wants you to be an imitator of Him then it is acceptable to show the feelings He created. Conversely, if you decide not to express your feelings, you are not following Christ or being "Christlike." The benefits you receive from expressing your feelings will outweigh the changes you must make. Look up the examples in the Bible and pray for God to help you express your emotions.

TEARS ARE IMPORTANT

If you are someone that does not cry, you need to realize the vital importance that crying brings to communicating your needs and healing your body and soul. William Fry, Ph.D., a biochemist in the psychiatry department at the St. Paul-Ramsey Medical Center in St. Paul, Minnesota, "believes that emotional distress produces toxic substances in the body and that crying helps remove them from the system. This may be why someone who is sad feels better after having a good cry..."[34] Frederic Flach, M.D., associate clinical professor of psychiatry at Cornell University Medical College states "Stress causes imbalance and crying restores balance ... It relieves the central nervous system of tension. If we don't cry, that tension doesn't go away."[35] Even the Bible describes many times how God pays special attention to your tears, "I waited patiently for the Lord; he turned to me and heard my cry," (Psalms 40:1), "The eyes of the Lord are on the righteous and his ears are attentive to their cry ..." (Psalms 34:15).

THE FOUR QUESTION TECHNIQUE

When feelings do not flow, your relationship will not grow.

Communicating your thoughts and feelings is fundamental to your emotional well-being and the healthy foundation of any relationship. One way to discover what you are thinking or feeling inside is to use the following four question technique.

Instructions: When you or someone else observes something is bothering you, ask these four simple questions. You may answer these questions on your own or have someone ask you these questions when you are upset.

Question 1. Have someone ask you or ask yourself:
WHAT IS GOING ON INSIDE?

If you have difficulty expressing emotions, you will have difficulty realizing there are feelings stirring up inside. As a result you may hold emotion inside for days and not realize it. This first question is used as a "red flag" to help you recognize that something bothers you. Oftentimes others will notice you are upset before you will see it in yourself. Give friends or family members permission to ask you this question when they notice that you are upset. If identifying emotions is very difficult, you may want someone to help you figure out the answers to each question. As you become sensitive to your own emotions, it will become easier to answer this first question.

Question 2. After you have answered the first question and identified that something is wrong, have someone ask you or ask yourself:
WHAT AM I FEELING (THINKING) INSIDE?

(NOTE: You may want to use the word "thinking" (instead of "feeling") with an unemotional person.)

In order to take control of your feelings, you must identify the thoughts or emotions that are going on inside, i.e., hurt, frustration, anxiety, anger, fear, etc. (to help you identify feelings, refer to the chart of faces in the appendix). If you have struggled with expressing feelings throughout your life, this may be the hardest question for you. Remember you were born with these feelings and you should be allowed to feel them. The task of identifying feelings may seem overwhelming at first, but the more you express yourself, the easier it becomes. The hardest part may be giving yourself permission to feel.

When you are asked this question, you need to play the role of a detective and find the feelings inside. When you identify the feelings allow yourself to release them by saying or writing down statements such as, "*I feel . . . hurt, angry, frustrated, scared*" etc.

Question 3. After you have answered the second question and identified what you feel, have someone ask you or ask yourself:
WHY DO I FEEL (THINK) THIS WAY?

Think back over the past one to eight hours to determine what circumstances may have taken place that would have triggered these feelings. Often daily events can trigger the emotions you have suppressed hours or days ago. You should say aloud or write down the answer to this question through statements such as, "*I feel angry because. . .*"

Question 4. After you have answered the third question and identified why you feel that way, you have the option to answer this question:
WHAT WILL I DO ABOUT THESE FEELINGS (THOUGHTS)?

This question is to help you find constructive ways to deal with the original issues that may be causing the feelings. For example, you may want to say or write out the answers to questions such as: *Who was involved? What happened to make me think this way? When did I start thinking this way? How long have I been thinking this way? What can I say or do to change what happened?*

Changing your behavior and the way you have expressed yourself for many years can be difficult. It is advisable to have a mate, family member, or trusted friend be an accountability partner and give that person permission to ask these four questions. If you are alone, answer these questions by writing in a journal or saying them aloud to yourself. These are very helpful questions to ask yourself while driving home after a frustrating day at work, after caring for the children, spending time in prayer, etc. If you cannot sleep because your mind is whirling around with troubling thoughts, use these questions to get rid of what is bothering you. As you answer the questions you will feel a natural release of pressure and stress that will help you endure the rest of the day. Whatever you do, *you must physically release your feelings* by verbalizing or writing down the answers. As you begin to release the feelings inside, you will break free from old patterns and begin to feel more of an inner peace.

WHAT IF I CANNOT FEEL ANYTHING?

If you cannot find your feelings, don't give up trying! Remember, you were born with emotions and you should be allowed to use them. Try these suggestions.

1. *Have someone help you identify your feelings:* When you cannot feel anything, you need someone to give suggestions about the feelings they see or hear from you. Others can often detect your feelings better than you can. Use the emotional face sheet in the appendix to help identify what you feel.

2. *Identify how your body is physically reacting:* If you still do not know what to feel, identify how your body is physically reacting. Do you have a stomachache, pounding heart, or tightness somewhere in your body when you are upset? When you identify those aches and pains, be a detective and search for what your body is telling you. For example,

if you become upset over a comment made by your spouse, look at the four questions to discover how you feel. You may realize that something is wrong, which answers question number one. However, if you get stuck on question number two because you have no idea how you feel, start playing detective to find how your body is reacting. Let's say you have a whirling feeling in your stomach. As a detective, you figure that must mean you're scared. That's it; you're scared! If you have a difficult time playing detective on your own, ask someone to help you discover what is going on inside as you describe your physical reactions. The more you answer these questions, the easier it will become.

WORDS OF ENCOURAGEMENT

Communicating your feelings with an unemotional mate can be one of the most difficult struggles in your relationship. However, don't let that struggle get the best of you. You may be trying to communicate the best way you know how, only to be misunderstood and unappreciated. Don't give up; you are not alone with your struggles. In spite of the way your mate communicates, the most important thing you can do is focus on identifying and releasing your own emotions. As you react differently than you have in the past, you will free yourself emotionally and your mate will eventually respond differently. You can make a difference; keep reading!

Personal Reflection
Remember to identify and express your emotions with these questions:
1. What is going on inside?
2. What am I feeling (thinking) inside?
3. Why do I feel (think) this way?
4. What will I do about these feelings (thoughts)?

≈

STUDY QUESTIONS

1. What does it mean to "Be imitators of God . . ." when it comes to your emotions?

2. Why do you have tears and how have you been able to express them?

3. How can you utilize the four questions in your personal life and with others?

4. What can you do if you cannot identify your feelings?

5. After reading this chapter, what additional insights have you learned about yourself and what else can you do to change how you communicate your thoughts and feelings?

19

HOW TO COMMUNICATE
WITH YOUR MATE

~

Whatever comes out of your mouth is the best
indicator of the condition of your heart.

Bill was repeatedly having difficulty communicating with his wife, Terri. From all the times Terri hadn't responded he could only assume she was becoming hard of hearing. So Bill decided to try a little test with Terri, without telling her. One evening while Terri was reading in the living room, Bill stood behind Terri on the far side of the room. Very quietly Bill whispered, "Can you hear me?" There was no response. Moving a little closer, he whispered again, "Can you hear me?" There was still no response. Quietly Bill edged closer and said the same words, but still no answer to his question. Finally, he moved right behind her and said in a louder voice, "Can you hear me now?" To his surprise she turned around and gave the irritated response, "For the fourth time, yes!"

This little story emphasizes how hard it may be to express feelings if your mate does not allow them to happen. Unemotional people often discourage, criticize, and belittle others that communicate feelings. The longer your emotions are discouraged the less safe and secure you will be to express what you think and feel. Expressing emotions is a God-given ability and should always be allowed in any relationship. It is important to note that even though screaming, angry outbursts, and verbal threats can be considered expressing emotions, these expressions are *not* appropriate and considered a form of emotional and verbal abuse. Let's learn new ways to express your feelings with an unemotional mate.

WHEN YOUR MATE BECOMES DEFENSIVE

Most people seem to have arguments or disagreements over trivial issues that often produce defensiveness. If someone becomes defensive when opinions and feelings are shared (especially when it's about you), it is difficult to know how to react. Let's have a friendly "discussion" about defensiveness.

A. The more insecure you are, the more defensive you become

Terri stepped back admiring the finishing touches from repairing a small section of wallpaper in the bathroom. It wasn't perfect but it was worth the few hours it took to complete a project that Bill could never get around to fixing. When Bill stepped into the bathroom that night, he took one look at Terri's handiwork and said loudly so Terri could hear in the other room, "I can't believe you did it like that. What were you thinking?" Feeling like a brick just hit her, Terri shot back in defense, "Someone's got to do the work because of your laziness! You never do anything around here!" Terri ran in the bedroom and slammed the door behind her.

Terri's defensive response was to counter what she believed to be a personal attack against her work. This type of defensive response is based on the belief that you must defend yourself against the other person. But when you think about it logically, when Terri defended herself she was actually admitting automatically that Bill was right and she was wrong. You may say, "Hey, wait a minute, Bill was the one that was wrong and he was the one that started it."

My response to you would be, "If Terri did nothing wrong, then why did she feel the need to defend herself by shooting back a nasty comment?" The reason for Terri's response was coming from her poor self-confidence and insecurity of what she had done. Bill's comment triggered Terri's own issues of insecurity.

If you receive any type of comment that challenges what you say or do, you will take those words like a sharp knife to the heart, especially if you do not feel good about yourself. The more insecure you are about yourself, the more you will become defensive and either shut down or fight back. You would not be able to believe in yourself or believe you completed the project to the best of your ability. In addition, it is a fact that no matter what anyone says, God already made you good enough and if you did your best, then what you accomplished is good enough. If Terri felt good about herself and believed she did the project to the best of her ability (no matter the outcome), she would not become defensive. Let me explain as you read further.

B. Those comments are only opinions

Whether you are receiving defensive comments or giving them, you need to know the truth to set you free. For example, when you receive rude comments or cutting remarks, the truth is, those comments are only the other person's opinion. To understand what I mean, answer these questions with yes or no:

Should each mate have the right to have an opinion? Yes or No?
Should each mate have the right to voice an opinion? Yes or No?

If you answered "yes" to each question (and that's what it should be), then you believe you and your mate are allowed to have and say an opinion. That means the rude comment from your mate is only their opinion. If that is the case, why are you defending yourself against your mate's opinion? If you feel good about yourself and believe you did the best you knew how, you shouldn't feel the need to defend what you have done or what you believe is right. Your opinion is good enough! Just remember, the comments from your mate are only opinions, and you have a choice to accept or not accept those opinions. If your mate shows disrespect with hurtful comments, you certainly should set some boundaries by saying you don't appreciate those comments.

Let's again look at what happened to Terri and Bill. This time we will see how Terri reacts because she feels good about her handiwork and is able to set some boundaries with Bill. When Bill stepped into the bathroom that night and said loudly, "I can't believe you did it like that. What were you thinking?" Terri realized Bill did not have a good attitude and responded by saying, "I spent a considerable amount of time on that project. I don't appreciate your comments. Considering what it looked like before, I think I did a pretty good job. I would appreciate you not criticizing my work." Terri believed she did the best job she could and believed it was good enough. She realized Bill was entitled to his own opinion and did not need to become emotionally affected by his opinion.

C. Do not "own" the opinions of your mate

You don't have control over what your mate says. However, you do have control over what you do with your mate's comments. You do have a choice whether to allow those opinions to wound you or whether you should disregard them. If you become personally offended each time your mate says something negative, you have emotional issues that are being triggered. If this is the case, you need to seek counseling for your own past hurts.

D. Take responsibility for your own response

Let's say your mate makes an insensitive comment or argues with you. If you become emotionally upset by shutting down or arguing back, it is *your* responsibility that you became upset. You must take responsibility for your own emotional response! If you are good enough, if you do things the best you can, if you deserve respect, if the words are only your mate's opinion, then why are you getting so upset? Again, the reason you are becoming upset is because your mate is triggering the emotional issues that you haven't dealt with.

If you receive a nasty comment from your mate, you have a choice how you let that nasty comment affect you. The more insecure you are from the hurts in your past, the more you will become defensive and either argue or shut down emotionally. The more you respond defensively with your mate, the more you will fire up your mate to defend his or her position.

When Terri became defensive, she shot back in response, "Someone's got to do the work because of your laziness! You never do anything around here!" Her words would serve to fire up Bill for an attack with another rude comment. Before you know it, the verbal mud slinging will continue with all kinds of hurtful words. The defensiveness will not stop unless someone can be mature enough to stop it. You need to be the more mature adult and know when to put an end to the verbal battling. In extreme cases of someone yelling obscenities, you need to draw the line by saying that you will not tolerate it and walk away if he or she will not listen. If your mate is hostile, violent, or threatening, get counseling for your situation.

E. Take responsibility for your reactions

Even if you did not like the words or the tone of the message, it is important to consider what the other person said. This is especially important if there is something for which you need to take responsibility. Take for example Terri's response to Bill in the second scenario, "I spent a considerable amount of time on that project. I don't appreciate your comments. Considering what it looked like before, I think I did a pretty good job. I would appreciate you not criticizing my work." Because Terri responded more maturely and set appropriate boundaries, Bill should have acted more maturely and taken responsibility for his own inappropriate comment about Terri's work. A mature response for Bill might have been, "Now that you mention it, my comment was out of line. I didn't realize how much work you put into this. I'm sorry for my comment."

You may say, "You don't understand, Craig. My mate makes hurtful comments all the time."

If that is the case, my response to you would be, "I am saddened for your situation. However, I am more saddened that you do not stand up to your mate's hurtful comments!" Regardless of what is said, you have a choice how you take your mate's comments and how you will in turn respond. Believe in yourself and stop wasting your breath trying to argue about something that is only a rude and thoughtless opinion. Even if you did argue in return, chances are your mate does not listen to what you say anyway. If you are drawn into arguments and cannot stop defending yourself, or your mate is verbally berating, seek counseling to learn how to deal with the situation.

F. Reviewing what you can do with negative comments:

1. When your mate complains or makes a negative comment, do not let those comments wound your heart. Remember, it's only an opinion.

2. Believe in what you know to be true about yourself, not the opinion of someone else. Get counseling if you do not know what to believe about yourself.

3. Do not personalize the hurtful words from others. Only respond to let them know what you will not tolerate (set boundaries). Do not defend yourself against another per-

son's opinion; you will rarely win against a person who is angry and/or responding defensively.

4. Take responsibility for your own emotional reaction.

5. The more you defend yourself, the more you will give your mate an occasion to continue arguing with you.

6. Use the four-question technique (found in the previous chapter) to deal with the emotion in yourself or your mate.

ALLOWING EMOTIONS TO BE EXPRESSED

Living with people that do not express emotions often forces members of the family to hide or push away their feelings and struggle to make the best of a bad situation. Not allowing family members to express their feelings will discourage communication and perpetuates the belief that their thoughts and feelings do not matter. To help encourage the expression of feelings, here are some guidelines for both partners:

1. **What the UNEMOTIONAL person should do to allow others to express emotions:**

When your emotional mate is upset (especially if he or she is upset about you), this is not a time to fix your mate or defend yourself. Just *keep your mouth closed* and listen. Keeping your mouth closed will be more valuable than anything you can do. Try these simple steps.

• When you see your mate is upset (i.e., sad, crying, unusually quiet), start with the four questions found in the previous chapter.

• When your mate tells you or shows you what he or she is feeling, *keep your mouth closed* while he or she is expressing their feelings. Just listen.

- After your mate is done expressing thoughts or feelings, make a comment about what you observe your mate is feeling or has said, such as, "You seem angry."

- In response to you, your mate will either get worse or get better with their emotions. *Keep your mouth closed* until your mate is done expressing feelings. Just continue to listen and do not become defensive (even if the issue is about you).

- Again, after your mate is done expressing thoughts or feelings, simply make another comment about what you observe your mate is feelings or saying.

- Always tell your mate (even if you do not want to) that you are glad they are able to express those thoughts or feelings. The more that is released, the faster the problem will be resolved and the better you will get along.

- Let your mate know you are sorry for making her or him feel that way. (If your mate says you are the reason for her or him being upset, you should apologize and work on stopping what made your mate upset.)

Here's an example how you can allow your partner to express feelings:

Emotional mate is looking sad, quiet, or withdrawn, with some tears.

Unemotional mate (commenting on what you observe): "You look sad right now. What's going on inside?"

Emotional mate says: "I'm upset at what you did yesterday. How could you be so rotten?"

Unemotional mate says: "It sounds like what I did really made you upset. What are you feeling?"

Emotional mate says (more upset): "You always do this;

I can't believe you said that in front of everyone. I hate it when you do that!"

Unemotional mate says (responds again to what you see or hear): "Wow, I didn't realize what I did was so upsetting to you. I should not have done that to you in front of everyone. I'm sorry."

Emotional mate (begins to cool off): "Well, I really wish you wouldn't do that in front of other people. It really hurts me."

Unemotional mate says (shows appreciation for the feelings): "I appreciate you letting me know how you feel. I'm sorry that I hurt you so much."

2. **How the EMOTIONAL person can express feelings with your unemotional mate:**

Unemotional people find it difficult to allow others to express feelings or thoughts. It is very difficult for the emotional mate to share his or her feelings with a defensive unemotional partner. When you need to share your thoughts or feelings with an unreceptive unemotional mate, the following steps may be used:

- Whatever the issue, you need to approach the unemotional mate with a word of encouragement for something he or she has done either related to the issue or something as close to it as possible. This may be a hard step to initiate, but it is crucial to opening the door to communications.

  ≈ To initiate communication with a man, make a comment about what *he does,* showing respect for his time, effort, or accomplishment. For example, "I could see you put a lot of time into putting that together; I do appreciate your effort."

≈ To initiate communication with a woman, make a comment about how much *you like* what she has done or give a compliment about her. For example, "What you did really looks nice." Or "It looks like you really put a lot of time into this."

- Proceed with a statement about how you feel using "I" statements and not statements that are accusatory or blaming. Try not to use statements that begin with the word "you."

- If your mate gets defensive (and chances are they will), do not argue back. Your comments, in return, will only fuel the insecurity of your mate.

- If your mate becomes defensive, be the more mature partner. Comment on what you see or hear and ask what they are thinking: "You seem upset. What are you thinking? Why are you thinking this way?"

- If your mate does not respond at that moment, back off. Once everything settles down (even if it is the next day), try again to state your feelings.

- If your mate has little or no response to your feelings, you need to: 1. Check to see if you are approaching your mate with a poor attitude. If you are approaching your mate with a respective, calm attitude and you still cannot say your feelings, you have a mate with a thick wall of hurt and pride that needs healing (and he or she is not aware of it). 2. Follow the steps in the next chapters to find ways to break down the wall that is not allowing feelings out.

Here's an example how you can try to express feelings with your unemotional partner:

Emotional mate says (starts with the positive respectful comment): "How was your time with the guys last night?

You seemed to have a good time." (Make sure you get rid of the angry tone).

Unemotional mate's reply: "It was okay; we watched a movie until two."

Emotional mate says (using an "I" or "me" statement): "I'm glad you had a good time. To be honest, it worries me when you are out so late. I miss having you here with me and the kids. It would make me feel better if you would come home earlier. Could you do that next time?"

The positive statement disarms your mate and does not automatically send him or her on the defensive. The "I" or "me" statement keeps the focus on you and decreases the defensiveness. Since insecure unemotional people can get defensive no matter what you say, don't be too surprised if you need to try this a few times before it works. Do not try to defend yourself when your mate is upset at you (unless you are threatened). Trying to verbally defend yourself will not get you anywhere. Remember, unemotional people will typically think about themselves and will often not hear what you are trying to communicate.

If you have been putting up with angry and defensive responses from your mate for years, this technique will take a lot of patience to find the right words to be positive. If you feel hurt and enraged because of how you have been treated, I strongly recommend you seek counseling to work on your own hurt.

WORDS OF ENCOURAGEMENT

Before you try to communicate your thoughts or feelings with others, you must learn to be confident and strong in identifying and expressing your own feelings. The more confident and secure you are with identifying what you feel inside, the less likely you will second guess your own thoughts and emotions if your mate criticizes what you say or feel. When you feel confident to express your own feelings, the more likely you will stand up for yourself and move forward with changing yourself. Remember that you are not alone in your struggles. Seek support from friends, God, and a counselor to build your confidence. "[God] gives strength to the weary and increases the power to the weak," (Isaiah 40:29).

Personal Reflection
May my thoughts and feelings be true to my heart.

≈

STUDY QUESTIONS

1. How are you responsible for your own defensive reaction?

2. Should you and your mate be allowed to have an opinion?

3. Should you take your mate's opinion personally? Explain your answer.

4. Describe what you should do with the opinion or comment of your mate?

5. What can the *unemotional mate* do to allow others to express emotions?

6. What can the *emotional mate* do to express feelings with the unemotional mate?

7. After reading this chapter, what additional insights have you learned about yourself and what else can you do to change how you express yourself?

20

IMPROVING THE RELATIONSHIP

~

*If you want the relationship to work, you
must work for the relationship.*

If you are going to make this relationship work, both partners need to work toward common goals. If you want to revive the relationship, here are some suggestions:

BE INTENTIONAL ABOUT SHOWING EMOTIONS AND AFFECTION

When you do not show emotions or affection, your mate interprets that as though you do not care. Early in our marriage, I remember one of my wife's frequent complaints was that I did not show enough affection. In one of my *I'll-try-harder* moments, believing I found the answer to all our problems, I said to my wife, "If you need a hug, just let me know."

Wondering where my head had been all these married years, my wife shot back, "If I have to ask for a hug, then your hug doesn't mean anything."

Feeling a little defeated by her answer, I threw back my reply, "Well, I don't know when you need a hug. I can't read your mind."

Becoming more irritated, my wife stated, "You're supposed to know. You married me, didn't you?" I knew I had better get out of this conversation quickly since I wasn't going to win anyway.

HUGS ARE THE BEST FORM OF SHARING AFFECTION

Since our conversation made me realize how meaningful hugs were for my wife (women do better with many tender touches each day), I decided to make a decision to start hugging her every day. This was not a small task for me since I was not the hugging type (I thought I was too macho). Since I really wanted to succeed, I had a brainstorm idea to put little sticky notes all over the house with the simple words, "Hug wife." My wife hated the idea at first, thinking, *You don't even love me enough to remember to hug me?* Over time she warmed up to the idea, realizing my working to remember hugs was not because I did not love her, but from my earnest desire to learn *how* to love her. As I gave an honest effort toward showing affection, my wife was more accepting and more loving in return.

I realized I had to make the decision to be different, and I could not let my shortcomings stop me from improving how I treated my wife. After several months of reminding myself to hug my wife, hugging became more natural. In fact, I eventually hugged my wife not because I had to, but because I actually enjoyed it! Imagine that! The more I held my wife in my arms, the more I learned to love and the more each of us softened inside. Both of us were encouraged.

GIVE MORE THAN WHAT YOU EXPECT TO RECEIVE

Women expect to receive love from the husband just as much as the man expects to receive respect from the wife. My wife wants me to give hugs and kisses just as much as I want praises for my accomplishments. *The bottom line is all about giving your mate more than what you expect to receive.* Unfortunately, the selfishness of the unemotional mate, combined with the resentment of the emotional partner, can hurt any chances for showing love or respect to one another. However, biblical common sense can go a long way. "Give, and it will be given to you. A good measure, pressed down, shaken together and running over, will be poured into your lap. For with the measure you use, it will be measured to you," (Luke 6:38). As the Bible states, when you give your mate what they need, you will get what you want. What will you choose to give?

REMINDERS TO EXPRESS YOURSELF

If you need a reminder to give acts of affection or to express your emotions, place a note anywhere in your home, office, or car. If your mate initially becomes irritated by the notes, tell him or her something like, "I have not shown love very well in the past and I really want to be different. I am trying whatever it takes to learn how to love you and I would really appreciate your understanding."

At first, your mate may interpret your new signs of affection as a bribe or an insincere form of change. Over time, as you consistently show signs of affection, your mate will be more accepting. However, the proof is in your change, not in your reminder notes. Your actions will prove your intentions. Whatever you choose, make the changes because you want to and not because you have to! You do have a choice and more control over the direction of this relationship than you believe. However, you must take the initiative to change. Oftentimes it is in the little things that you do (on a regular basis) that really matter. Try these expressions of affection for your mate:

≈ Say, *I love you*
≈ Clean your mate's car
≈ Give a call for no reason
≈ Give words of appreciation
≈ Make dinner for your family
≈ Take your mate to dinner

≈ Clean the house
≈ Compliment your mate
≈ Leave a kind note
≈ Go food shopping
≈ Give a hug; give a kiss

GIVE GRACE TO YOUR MATE

If you are the emotional mate living with a partner that is unemotional, you may sometimes feel like you're living with an alien from another planet. If your unemotional partner is willing to try to make some changes, give him or her some grace. The type of grace needed is the favor, goodwill, or acts of kindness for the *attempts* being made. Notice that I wrote the word *attempts*. Your mate will be making attempts, but you will be expecting perfection. After all, you may say, "He should know what I want because I've been telling him for years." Even if you have been waiting a long time to be loved, you need to come along side your mate as he or she makes an effort to change. You may ask, "Why should I give grace to a person who has not given what I needed in the first place?" My response is for you to take this moment and think logically (rather than emotionally), when answering these questions:

1. Would your mate intentionally choose to live unemotional for the rest of his or her life?

2. Did your unemotional mate intentionally marry you to purposely make you unhappy?

3. Is your mate "unemotional" on purpose, as if he or she likes to be this way?

4. Do you believe your unemotional mate wants to hurt you on purpose?

Most likely your answers are "no" because you realize from a logical point of view, it doesn't make sense why your mate behaves this way. It doesn't make sense because many of the behaviors of an upset, unemotional person typically do not make sense. Do not let the anger from how you have been treated over the years get in the way of allowing your mate to succeed at some things and fail at others. The grace you give may be what is needed to help your mate succeed and ultimately help your relationship to succeed. The greatest reason for giving your mate grace is because someone needs to be the more mature adult in your dysfunctional relationship. More importantly, God expects you to give grace. Colossians 3:13 reminds you to, "Bear with each other and forgive whatever grievances you may have against one another. Forgive as the Lord forgave you." In spite of what your mate has done, you have a choice to get better or a choice to stay bitter.

ACCEPTING CHANGES BY THE EMOTIONAL MATE

If your unemotional mate is willing to make the changes you have desired (and prayed about) for so long, believe it or not, you may have a hard time accepting those changes. After years of waiting for your unemotional mate to love you, there may be so much resentment, distrust, hurt, and anger that you may be too hurt to accept the very thing you have always wanted.

However, you may ask, "After all these years of not loving me, why should I start loving him (or her) now?" There are some important reasons to accept the changes. If you reject the changes now, you are rejecting the very thing you've always wanted, throwing away all that you invested to this point. If you do not learn how to accept what your changing mate gives to you, you will continue to be unhappy and only know how to live in dysfunctional relationships. The most important reason to accept the changes is because God expects you to forgive. Not because you may want to forgive, but because it is what the more mature, secure, person needs to do. Ephesians 4:31–32 reminds you to, "Get rid of all bitterness, rage and anger, brawling and slander, along with every form of malice. Be kind and compassionate to one another, forgiving each other, just as in Christ God forgave you."

WHEN THE EMOTIONAL MATE HAS DIFFICULTY ACCEPTING LOVE

It is very common for an emotional mate, who is so accustomed to acting as the pursuer or fixer of the relationship, to reject the new efforts of the unemotional mate. As odd as it sounds, the emotional mate probably does not know how to accept someone who actually begins to show love, especially if love has not been given for years. This response is similar to what you read in the chapter "Dancing the Relationship Tango." If you begin to push away what your unemotional mate is trying to give you, I strongly suggest you see a counselor to work through your own issues.

Suggestions for the emotional mate to help the unemotional partner:

- Find ways to let go of your negative emotions to help you provide grace.

- Begin daily prayer and ask how God wants you to change, rather than how you can change your mate.

- Stop nagging your mate. They know very well what you want. Your nagging only reveals your own insecurity and creates increased resentment toward you.

- Reward the positive and ignore the negative. Give a word of encouragement when your mate says or shows something positive and say little or nothing when your mate says or shows something negative.

- When your mate reverts back to his or her old ways, do not give the old, "I told you so," lecture. You must step back emotionally and physically. If you pay less attention or ignore your mate, they will get the picture better than a thousand words. If you have always shut down (instead of nagging) when something negative happened, you can say what you feel using a short, firm, calm, "I" statement. Direct and brief comments from a formerly quiet person is also better than a thousand words.

- Frequently identify and express your feelings through talking to a friend, praying, or writing in a journal. It is very important that you routinely let out your feelings. If you don't let out your hurts and frustrations in a positive way, they will come out in way you may regret.

- Seek counseling for emotional support and healing

PUT AWAY THE OLD SELF AND PUT ON THE NEW SELF

It would be unfair to ask anyone to make a change unless they knew how to change from an old way of life to a new way of living. The best place to start finding information regarding how you should change is from the biblical wisdom of Chapter 4 of Ephesians and Chapter 5 of Galatians. The best way to change into the new self is to allow God to help you by accepting Him into your life. When you accept Jesus Christ into your heart, you are "a new creation; the old has gone, the new has come," (2 Corinthians 5:17).

Take off old	Put on new	Bible verse
•Being deceitful	•New attitude	•Eph. 4:22, 23
•Lying	•Speak truthfully	•Eph. 4:25
•Angry at others	•Do not be angry	•Eph. 4:26
•Unwholesome talk	•Build up others	•Eph. 4:29
•Bitterness, rage, anger, brawling slander, malice	•Kind, forgiving, compassionate	•Eph. 4:31, 32

Living with your unhealthy habits and attitudes is the destructive part of your old nature that will destroy any good that you try to foster in yourself and your relationship. You want to break free of the unhealthy old self and change toward a healthy new self. The Bible is clear about what happens to those that indulge in the old nature and clear what happens when you become a new creation with the help of Christ in your heart. "I warn you, as I did before, that those who live like this will not inherit the kingdom of God," (Galatians 5:21). "Those who belong to Christ Jesus have crucified the sinful nature with its passions and desires," (Galatians 5:24).

Take off old	*Put on new*	*Bible verse*
•Indulging in sin	•Serve in love	•Gal. 5:13
•Destroying others	•Love other	•Gal. 5:14, 15
•Sexual immorality, impurity, rage, idolatry, envy, hatred, discord, jealousy, factions, witchcraft, debauchery, drunkenness, selfish ambition,	•Love, joy, peace, patience, kindness, goodness, faithfulness, self-control, gentleness	•Gal. 5:19–23

PRAYER

Write down the following prayers on a card. Pray and meditate on the words throughout the day:

1. Pray for yourself: *Dear Lord, give me a new heart and put a new spirit in me; remove my heart of stone and give me a heart of flesh.*

2. Pray for your mate: *Dear Lord, give (mate's name) a new heart and put a new spirit in him (or her); remove the heart of stone and give (mate's name) a heart of flesh.*

Putting away the old self can be hard to do if you have been living with those unhealthy issues all your life. However, you can do it with the help of prayer, counseling, and positive emotional support from friends. The best way to put away the old and put on the new is by asking Christ for help with this prayer. *Dear Jesus, I realize I have done wrong and I need you to guide me to do right. Forgive me of my sins and cleanse my heart. Come into my heart as my Lord and Savior, in Jesus Christ's name I pray.* Write down the date you prayed and tell someone about your decision.

WORDS OF ENCOURAGEMENT

If there is an attempt to improve the relationship, you have the potential to make positive changes happen. If you attempt to bring the relationship together involving God in the process, you have the potential for something even greater to happen. "I will heal my people and let them enjoy abundant peace and security," (Jeremiah 33:6). If you are still struggling in your relationship, hang in there. Continue to pray and don't give up. The following chapters will bring more information for more drastic measures to help in your situation.

Personal Reflection
God, help me to renew my heart
and mind into what you want me to be.

STUDY QUESTIONS

1. What needs to change in you to put away the old self?

2. What needs to change in you to put on the new self?

3. Describe what the unemotional mate needs to do to show emotions and affection.

4. What must you do if you want the relationship to work?

5. What expressions of affection would your mate benefit from?

6. Why should the emotional mate have grace and describe how you can give it.

7. What are the characteristics of someone having a hard time accepting change and how would it be difficult to accept change?

8. After reading this chapter, what additional insights have you learned about yourself and what can you do to change your relationship for the better?

21

SHOWING LOVE AND RESPECT

~

Women want love, men want respect.
Without this there will be no contentment.

You've read those stories where the damsel dreams of the knight in shining armor that comes to rescue her from the clutches of the evil dragon. The damsel calls out into the darkness hoping someone will hear and rescue her. Suddenly, a handsome knight appears out of the forest and challenges the evil dragon. As a fight begins, the cunning wit and brute strength of the knight slays the evil dragon and wins the heart of the damsel. The knight sweeps up the damsel safely in his strong yet gentle arms, placing her on the back of his horse. The damsel has fallen in love with the knight as he has fought bravely for her freedom. They kiss and ride off into the sunset.

Wow, what a beautiful story! (Hand me the tissues!) Women dream of a knight in shining armor that will take them away and protect them from the evils of life. In fact, having someone pursue you and fight for you is what romance is often about. The woman wants to be special to someone and feel worth fighting for. It's easier to be in love with someone that wants you and treats you like a queen. It would be more natural to continue to feel love as long as the knight was there to protect the damsel from the harshness of life.

Every man in a relationship is looking for something to accomplish and feel proud about, like John Wayne or Tom

Cruise who fought for their women and triumphed over evil. In the beginning you fought for your mate and eventually won her love; what happened? Are you fighting *for* her love or fighting *against* her about something else? Most relationships start out with each person treating the other with love and respect, like you are a king or queen. However, once you conquer your spouse, you move on to conquer something else, like your career, children, or higher education. Your battles turn into something else: the strain of your job, the pull of the children, expectations of your spouse, or financial pressures. Each battle you fight robs your energy and attention away from fighting for your relationship.

To all you men, the damsel in your life still wants you to fight for her. She was dreaming about someone like you fighting for her even before you appeared in her life. She is still dreaming about you fighting for her love and making the relationship a priority in your life. If you show her the love she wants, she will in turn show you the respect you want.

To all you women, the knight in your life still believes he is fighting a battle. Unfortunately, the battle may not be to sweep you off your feet. The man in your life needs to feel that you still appreciate his fighting for whatever he is trying to accomplish. When you respect the good that he has done, you will get the love you want. Plain and simple, when the man does not show love to the women, the woman does not show respect to the man. Let's explore how to give love and respect.

RELATIONSHIPS ARE A MATTER OF THE HEART

Relationships are about giving and receiving love and respect. Sadly, most of you reading this do not know what a healthy, loving relationship looks or feels like. Quite frankly, when you put the other person first, you always win. If you are putting yourself first, you will always lose. Here are some suggestions to put your mate first:

1. "Do nothing out of selfish ambition or vain conceit, but in humility consider others better than yourselves. Each of you should look not only to your own interests, but also to the interests of others. Your attitude should be the mind as that of Christ Jesus," (Philippians 2:3–5).

   - Let your mate know when you are running late or your plans change.

   - Here is the order of life that you must live by:
     Put God first in all things
     Put family second (spouse first; children second)
     Put career third
     Put yourself last

   - Take time to listen to your mate when making a decision.

   - On your way home from work, do not plan what *you* want to do. You must be flexible and consider what the family wants to do. No matter how hard you have worked all day, if you have a mate and family, your responsibility is to take care of their needs when you get home. If you do not take care of your spouse and family, everyone and everything else will suffer.

   - You must adjust your personal agenda and work responsibility to fit your spouse and family. You can always get another job, but you don't want to lose your family.

   - Be mindful and understanding of your mate's emotions. When your mate does or does not express emotions, just make a calm, caring comment about what you observe. For example, if your mate starts to cry, you may say, "You seem sad right now." If your mate shuts down, you may say, "You seem quiet, is there anything on your mind?" If you do not know what to say, just comment on what you see happening with the other person. This is also an excellent method to use with children.

2. "Each one of you also must love his wife as he loves himself, and the wife must respect her husband," (Ephesians 5:33).

Men want to be respected and women want to be loved. Men will tend to work alone on projects and find a sense of accomplishment in what he does with the project. As a result, men will tend to show love through what he accomplishes on his own with projects or tasks. Men want to receive respect through your acknowledgement of what he has accomplished.

Women on the other hand like to be with others and find love through the relationship that is established while accomplishing the project. Women will also tend to show love through doing things for others and receive love from the relationship that is established while doing those things. Be aware that this description of these needs is not the same for everyone. Some women would benefit from acknowledgement of what they accomplish and some men would enjoy doing things with others.

The wife needs to show appreciation to the husband through words of praise, such as, "good job, thanks for fixing that," or "that was a good suggestion." The man needs to show love by doing things with his wife and giving acts of love such as, tender touches, listening without judgment, and verbal words of compassion ("I love you; I appreciate you"). Ephesians 5:33 is clear about what must happen to develop a healthy relationship. If the man does not show love, the woman typically will not want to show respect. If the woman does not show respect, the man typically will not show love. Who will be mature enough to give what the spouse needs? When the man receives respect he believes (feels) the woman cares about him.

When a woman receives signs of love, she feels the man cares about her.

Ways men can show love through words and actions:

Pray for her

Buy flowers or special card

Bring dinner home

Say, "I love you"

Compliment her

Open the car door for her

Give a back rub

Ask about her day

Hold her for no reason

Be romantic

Serve breakfast in bed

Take a walk with her

Go to dinner

Call her when you're at work

Clean the house

Clean the house again

Sit down and talk with her

Thank her for what she does

Wash the car

Watch her TV show with her

Hold hands in public

Ways women can show respect through words and actions:

Pray for him

Ask about his day

Hold him often

Pack a lunch

Watch sports with him

Give a loving look

Compliment him

Thank him for what he does

Show interest in his hobby

Don't be negative

Give a back rub

Make a favorite meal

Women, help your mate learn what makes you feel loved by writing a letter:

> *Dear* _____,
>
> *I want you to know how much I appreciate when you (*list what he does*). I know I have not been telling you lately so I wanted to let you know. I also wanted you to know it makes me feel good when you show me or tell me that you love me. I really feel loved when you (*mention things he does that you like*). I have realized when you show me love that I have more of a*

desire to give love back to you. Thank you for your willingness to show me love.

Love, _____

Men, help your mate learn what makes you feel respected by writing a letter:

Dear _____,

*I want you to know how much I appreciate when you (*list what she does*). I know I have not been telling you lately so I wanted you to know. I also wanted you to know I like it when you show me or tell me how much you appreciate something I have done. I feel appreciated when you (*mention things she does that you like*). I have realized when you appreciate me that I have more of a desire to give back to you. Thank you for your willingness to show me appreciation.*

Love, _____

3. "When I was a child, I talked like a child; I thought like a child, I reasoned like a child. When I became a man, I put childish ways behind me," (1 Corinthians 13:11).

As an adult, take responsibility for your own actions and behaviors. If your mate says or does something that you do not like, do you blame your mate and have an emotional outburst or shut down emotionally? Who is responsible for your behavior? You are! Most arguments are started from disagreements about small issues that get blown out of proportion. When you are hurt inside from something your mate has said, take responsibility for your own reactions. If you are afraid to stand up to your mate, find out what makes you afraid. If you emotionally shut down and go into your own cave, you need to find out why. If you become angry and defensive when you are questioned, it is your responsibility to find out why. When you were a child, you talked like a child, thought like a child, and behaved like a child. Now that you are an adult, what is your excuse for behaving like a child? You need to stop having angry outbursts, walking away, or shutting down emotionally like a child and stop blaming your mate and everyone else for your childish behavior. Look at your behavior and take responsibility for yourself. If you cannot stop on your own, you need to seek professional counseling.

ASK WHAT YOU NEED FROM EACH OTHER

When you live in a home without emotion, there tends to be little (or no) conversation about personal needs. Without conversation about personal needs, you probably do not know what what your mate needs emotionally, socially, physically, and spiritually, which means your relationship is suffering. If you want to make a difference try this exercise:

1. **On separate papers you and your mate should write the answers to these questions:**

   a. When I am sad and show tears, I need my mate to:

   b. When I am angry or frustrated, I need my mate to:

   c. When I disagree, I need my mate to:

   d. When I want to talk or ask for time together, I need my mate to:

   e. When I look or act tired and stressed out, I need my mate to:

2. **Exchange what you have written with your mate and do the following:**

   a. Read the question and answers you have received from your mate.

   b. Explain what you believe your mate wrote on the paper. If you misunderstand your mate's answers, ask your mate to explain what was written.

WORDS OF ENCOURAGEMENT

The best way to improve your relationship is for a man to love his wife and woman to respect her husband. You need to take the initiative to help your mate learn what you need. Even if you have already told your mate these things a thousand times, make this a thousand and one. Do not expect your mate to know exactly what you want and do not use this time to criticize your mate because they don't understand you. God created you differently to be a helpmate not a hindrance. You need to be mature enough to see and accept that difference.

Personal Reflection

Lord, help me to accept the difference of my mate, and help me find ways to show love and respect.

STUDY QUESTIONS

1. What can you do to help your mate believe they are first in your life?

2. Describe how you show (or do not show) love and respect to your mate.

3. Describe how you can improve showing love and respect to one another.

4. After reading this chapter, what additional insights have you learned about yourself and what can you do to change your life and your relationship for the better?

PART IV

making radical changes

22

WHAT TO DO WHEN YOUR MATE DOES NOT CHANGE

—

*Do not let what you want get in the
way of what you really need.*

Chris told Ruth he would be home for dinner by five o'clock. Just before he was ready to leave the office, a phone call detained him longer than expected. Chris arrived home twenty-five minutes late to see his family sitting at the kitchen table finishing their dinner. Ruth's eyes threw daggers at Chris as she said with anger, "Why are you so late? You always do this to me!"

Chris felt up against a wall without a blindfold ready for execution. Caught off guard, Chris said in his feeble defense, "I'm not always late. I wasn't late yesterday." There were a few more words said before Chris sat down to eat his dinner alone. The tension was so uncomfortable Chris knew he could not go to bed with the hostility between them.

Before the night was over, Chris again tried to explain why he was late for dinner. In her anger Ruth said, "It's always the same thing. You're not there for me."

Chris said in his *narrow-minded defensive way,* "What do you mean I'm not there for you? I don't come home late every night. I came home on time last night." Ruth frowned even more, realizing the *thick-headed* part of his maleness wasn't getting it. As always, Chris was just trying to defend himself, not wanting to look bad or feel any worse than he already did. He quickly added, "When I come home I'm there for you—I'm around."

Ruth countered with a disappointed voice, "Yeah, it's always the same. You're in the house but not with me. You're doing something else like on the computer or working in the garage. I'm tired of it and do not want to live this way anymore."

As Ruth walked away, Chris sensed she was upset, but he really didn't want to find out how angry she was. Deep down Chris knew there was some truth to what Ruth was saying, but he really didn't understand what she wanted and his stubbornness did not let him give in. What was different about Ruth was her standing up for herself and ending the conversation before the "discussion" got too far out of hand. Ruth was showing signs of being fed up with the relationship, which made Chris realize he needed to do something different or the situation would only get worse. It was like a small voice was saying to Chris, *You better swallow your pride and make some changes or you'll lose something more important than just your pride.*

SECTION I:
CHANGE OR SUFFER THE CONSEQUENCES

Sadly, my office schedule is filled with couples like Ruth and Chris where one mate is totally fed up because the other mate does not show love and respect. However, it often gets to the point where one partner wants out of the relationship because no positive changes are taking place. I do all I can to direct each relationship toward a healthier path of reconciliation. Unfortunately, there comes a point in time where one mate is so emotionally devastated, little can be salvaged until a major overhaul and restoration can be done. The more discontent and hurt a mate has in his or her heart, the more he or she will pull away. In an emotionless relationship, one mate is emotionally distant and the other mate has been unsuccessfully trying to get emotionally close for some time (probably years). Both are unsatisfied and living in a dry, barren relationship. This way of life is not living; it is only existing as you slowly die inside.

SUFFERING THE CONSEQUENCES

If you are like Ruth, you may be trying to get across a message that is a plea for the attention or respect you desperately desire. If you are unemotional like Chris and you don't know how to change, you have to make a decision to be different. The unemotional mate must become intentional about making personal changes, not for the emotional mate, but because you believe it is necessary and the only thing to do. If the unemotional mate does not make an effort to change, chances are he or she will lose more than they could ever realize. The unemotional mate must either change or suffer the consequences if he or she does not change. The consequences can be different depending on the extent of damage the relationship has suffered. If the unemotional mate does not change, he or she will continue to:

- Not get what he or she wants.
- Give a message that he or she doesn't care (which will hurt the emotional mate even more, making him or her feel less loved).
- Increase the complaining, nagging, and criticizing from the emotional mate because of the lack of love.
- Increase the chances the mate will stop listening to you, shut down emotionally, and/or become even more distant.
- Increase the chances the emotional mate (and children) will leave (and not come back).
- Show the children he or she doesn't care about the relationship.

As the unemotional mate, if you do not change, you will be more responsible for the devastating consequences of the relationship. Let me say it again: if you do not change, you *will* have consequences. The consequences that may happen are not only a threat they are a promise! What and when something will happen is up to you and the relationship you foster with your family members. If you do not begin the process of change, there is a larger potential for you to lose everything that is important to you. Unfortunately, over fifty percent of American first time married couples divorce and over seventy percent of second time married couples divorce. Do you want to be the next casualty and lose everything you have invested so far? Do you want to suffer (more) consequences? Chances are your emotional mate wants a relationship with you (no matter how much complaining he or she does). Stop blaming what is happening on everyone or everything else and take responsibility for what you must do to improve yourself and your relationship. You do have a choice whether to change yourself and your circumstances.

THE UNEMOTIONAL MATE HAS NO REASON TO CHANGE

In all the years Ruth either complained or gave love, there were little improvements in Chris's behavior for her efforts. In fact, the more Ruth complained, the more Chris would stop listening and blame her for the problems. Ruth felt frustrated that her efforts could not make the changes she so desperately desired.

When I explained to Ruth that her efforts to change Chris were not working because he had no reason to change, Ruth looked dumbfounded. "What do you mean, 'No reason to change'? He should change because he loves me," Ruth said with conviction. I told Ruth that is among the biggest problems facing emotionless relationships. Often, the emotional mate (usually the wife) loves with a giving heart and expects the unemotional mate to do the same. This perception starts before marriage, with the belief love will prevail and the marriage bond will overcome all problems. There is a predominant belief with women that a man's willingness to marry automatically means he knows how to show love in a marriage. Unemotional people do not have the same concept of love and do not know how to love the way the emotional mate dreams of being loved. Even though this truth rarely hits home until after the wedding, the emotional partner will continue to work hard, hoping that someday the dream will come true. It becomes even more hurtful when the unemotional mate does not respond to the years of verbal requests to change. Here are some explanations why the unemotional mate does not change.

When kindness does not change your mate

Even though serving your mate with kindness is important, trying to change an emotionally dead mate with kindness can bring opposite results. Let me explain. Ruth always acted with the belief that "killing with kindness" or being submissive would change the undesirable behavior. However, often the opposite would happen with Chris. Since the unemotional mate is self-focused and has a 'what's in it for me' attitude, giving kindness only reinforces the belief of being in control and encourages the expectation the world revolves around them. When Chris emotionally shut down or yelled after a disagreement, Ruth would always be the peacemaker by taking the initiative to make things better with Chris.

If you use kindness to keep the peace or rescue the relationship, your act of kindness can actually serve to reinforce the unhealthy behavior. Your kindness only serves to pardon the person who hurt you from taking responsibility to do anything about their behavior. Trying to change unhealthy behaviors with kindness only serves as a seal of approval regarding the unhealthy behaviors and reinforces the expectation that you are obligated to give kindness. For example, let's say Chris has a long term habit of irritable moods, creating either outbursts of emotion or isolating himself from the family. For years Ruth would walk on eggshells if Chris would become upset or withdraw into his shell. As a result, Ruth would constantly try to make things right, keep the peace, or work hard to prepare the home and kids to decrease anything that would potentially upset Chris. If Chris became upset around the kids, she would make excuses for him. Unfortunately, all the extra work and keeping the peace never really worked because Chris continued to find something to get upset about. Not only was Ruth allowing Chris to get away with disrespectful behavior, she was excusing Chris from taking any responsibility with his own unhealthy behaviors. Regardless of the issue, having to walk on eggshells in your own home is nothing short of emotional abuse.

Instead, Ruth needs to stop trying to fix the situation with her kindness and become aware of her own feelings (use the four question technique you learned earlier) when Chris gets upset. Ruth needs to build her own confidence level (if she is afraid of Chris) through prayer, emotional support, and professional help to change how she is responding to Chris. Ruth needs to calmly make a comment either at the time Chris becomes upset or the next day. Something like, "You seem upset right now." Wait for a response. Then say, "I realize you are upset, but I don't feel I deserve to be treated that way." Or, "It hurts me when you say that, and I do not want you to say that anymore."

It would be important to note that changing how you use

kindness with an unemotional mate may be contradictory to what you have learned as a Christian. Everyone should continue to give kindness as it states in the Bible, "Be kind and compassionate to one another . . ." (Ephesians 4:32). However, Jesus also was bold and straightforward about chastising those that took advantage of others. Be wise with how you are being treated and do not allow unhealthy words or behaviors to continue toward you, "So, watch yourselves. If your brother sins, rebuke him, and if he repents, forgive him," (Luke 17:3). It is not a sin to stand up for what is right or to set boundaries in order for people to know what you will and will not accept. This is what respect is all about.

When anger does not change your mate

Expressions of anger toward the unemotional mate can be shown in forms of nonverbal gestures, verbal outbursts, throwing things, slamming doors, and other forms of passive aggressive actions, such as, not making dinner, leaving, locking doors, denying pleasures, etc. These expressions can serve to ignite the unemotional mate's fury or force them to retreat into an isolated, silent world. The unemotional mate relies on the behaviors of others to use as reasons to blame or excuse his or her own unhealthy behaviors. When Ruth became upset by Chris's sarcastic remarks, Chris would use Ruth's behavior against her by saying, "You're no Christian, look at how you're acting." The anger from someone else is often all the excuse the unemotional person needs to ignite a flurry of blame and anger.

The Bible is clear that you are allowed to be angry, but you are not to let the anger get to a point where it will hurt others or make someone else stumble in their faith. "In your anger do not sin: Do not let the sun go down while you are still angry, and do not give the devil a foothold," (Ephesians 4:26–27). In order to become angry appropriately, first recognize that unhealthy anger only makes things worse and is only the sign of insecurity. Verbalize your anger appropriately using words that describe how you feel, rather than being out of control using outbursts of emotion that hurt others. The Bible is clear about anger, "A fool gives vent to his anger, but a wise man keeps himself under control," (Proverbs 29:11).

When tears do not change your mate

As you have learned, tears should be a natural, God-given emotional response. However, the unemotional person does not like to see emotion in his or her mate. The reason is because the expression of emotion from the emotional partner often stirs up insecurity, guilt, blame, fear, or resentment in the unemotional mate. Unemotional people do not understand emotion, do not like to see emotion, and of all things, do not want to be blamed for the emotion coming out of someone else. However, preventing anyone from expressing their God-given right to express appropriate emotion is degrading, hurtful, oppressive, and abusive. If the emotional mate cannot freely express emotion because of these reasons he or she should find ways to safely release emotions through writing, talking to a friend, praying aloud with God, or seeking counseling.

Personal Reflection

May my eyes be opened to the changes I need to see;
my heart be opened to the changes I need to feel;
my mind be opened to the changes I need to make.

≈

STUDY QUESTIONS

1. What are the consequences if a person does not change his or her unemotional life?

2. Describe reasons why your unemotional mate will not change.

3. Describe what happens when kindness, anger, or tears are expressed with the unemotional mate.

4. After reading this chapter, what additional insights have you learned about yourself and what can you do to change your situation for the better?

SECTION II
GET BETTER OR GET BITTER

Anyone living in an emotionless relationship will accumulate many normal emotions such as hurt, rejection, loneliness, and sadness. The longer you hold in these negative emotions, the longer you are being held hostage to those unhealthy emotions. If you think your mate is "making" you feel this way, you're wrong. The only thing your mate is doing is reacting in the manner he or she knows how, as a result of their own negative issues in their life. Even if you are the victim of their insensitive words or actions that come at you during the heat of the moment, you still have the choice what to do with those comments. You have a choice to hold in or let go of the very emotion that is keeping you miserable. You must decide what to do with those emotions. This may be the hardest thing for you to do right now, but it will be the best thing you can do to free yourself from what you feel your mate is putting you through.

CHOOSING TO BECOME BETTER OR BITTER

To ultimately have a better relationship, you must *decide* to take charge of your own emotions to have a better frame of mind and a better outlook on life. You must decide to do something with your hurt and anger or else hurt and anger will do something to you. When you harbor negative feelings in your heart the relationship does not have a chance to change. The Bible is the best guide to learn what you are to do with negative emotions. "Get rid of all bitterness, rage and anger, brawling and slander, along with every form of malice. Be kind and compassionate to one another, forgiving each other, just as in Christ God forgave you," (Ephesians 4:31,32). As long as you hold on to these unhealthy emotions, you will:

- Be controlled by your mate. "He who angers you controls you."
- Remain a slave (in bondage) to the negative emotions and turmoil whirling inside.
- Increase risk of physical illnesses (aches/pains, fatigue, insomnia, etc.).
- Increase risk of emotional illness (anxiety, anger, fears, depression, etc.).
- Increase risk of allowing your negative emotions to fuel sinful acts and behaviors.
- Increase risk of losing/damaging more in your life (finances, relationships, etc.).
- Struggle with trusting others—even God.

A. To help with your negative emotions, begin with this exercise. Sit in a quiet place away from distractions. As you think about your life and your relationship up to this point in time, write down any emotions that you have experienced. (You can use the emotional faces found in the appendix.)

B. Let go of the emotions by praying the following with each emotion: "Dear God, I am holding in the emotion of (name the emotion). God, help me let go of this emotion and forgive me for holding it in my heart. Thank you for helping me. In the name of Jesus."

C. Write a detailed letter regarding how you think and feel about your mate and the relationship. You do not need to send the letter to your mate. Include the following in the letter:

1. What you originally dreamed this relationship would be like.

2. Your thoughts and feelings about how the relationship turned out differently.

3. What your mate has done over the years (still does) that has been negative (hurtful, disappointing, scary, etc.).

4. How you *felt* when your mate treated you that way (make sure you use feeling words).

5. How you would like the relationship to be different.

6. What emotions or events you can (or cannot) give to God to begin letting go and moving toward forgiveness.

D. Read the finished letter aloud to a friend or aloud to God. If you want to tell your mate what you wrote, I recommend you write the letter again to organize your thoughts better.

E. Give the letter to God. You may pray: "Dear God, I give you this letter with all my feelings. Help me not to take them back. In the name of Jesus."

F. You can rip up the letter into tiny pieces as a symbol of letting it go.

NOTE: Writing this letter does not mean you will never again have negative emotions. It means you are beginning to let go of the past negative emotions you have accumulated against your mate. From this point forward, when you have negative emotions use the questions to identify your emotions: *What is going on inside? What am I feeling? Why am I feeling this way? What am I going to do about these feelings?*

WHEN YOU ARE NOT ABLE TO LET GO

If you are like many mates that have been hurt by the unemotional partner, you may not want to let go of your hurt for a variety of reasons. Holding the emotion inside will only slow down or deteriorate the healing process and ultimately make it more difficult for you and the relationship to change for the better. Whatever the reason, I recommend you work with a counselor to guide you through the healing. Here are some reasons why many people have difficulty letting go of negative feelings:

I'm too angry to give in

If you are angry for the way you have been treated, letting go would be like giving in, letting them win, or letting your guard down. Your emotion blinds your ability to logically see you are not in control when you stay angry. There is an old saying, "He who angers you, controls you." The longer you are angry, the longer you stay in misery and the longer your mate takes advantage of you by controlling you. Do some soul searching and determine where the anger comes from and begin letting it go.

If I let go, I may get hurt again

If you have been repeatedly hurt in relationships (including father, mother) you will not want to be hurt again. As you learned earlier in the book, the first time you are hurt you may build a wall to protect yourself. With each subsequent hurt, you add more bricks to the wall until you have a huge fortress of protection. As a result, you will not feel safe letting your guard down if you feel even an ounce of concern you may be hurt again. The bottom line is, if you feel threatened or unsafe by the person you are with, you will not feel free to let go of your emotions. If you feel unsafe in the relationship, you need to take the steps to separate yourself emotionally and physically, found earlier in the book.

I'm waiting for my mate to change

If you are waiting for your mate to change before you make changes in your relationship you may be waiting forever. As long as you are being treated with disrespect, you are destined to live in an unsatisfying relationship. The longer you "wait" for an unemotional person, the longer you are enabling them to remain the same. The next chapter will address this issue in more detail.

You need to make changes to improve yourself and stop waiting or being dependent on someone or something to make those changes. You must take responsibility for what you can do to improve yourself. Begin to identify emotions deep inside and release them through journaling, prayer, and counseling. God is always ready and willing to hear about your hurts. "Though you have made me see troubles, many and bitter, you will restore my life again; from the depths of the earth you will again bring me up. You will increase my honor and comfort me once again," (Psalm 71:20–21).

Personal Reflection
God, help me to identify the negative feelings
I hold in my heart and help me let them go.

≈

STUDY QUESTIONS

1. How are negative emotions affecting you emotionally, socially, physically, and spiritually?

2. Describe the reasons why you have not made changes up to this point.

3. After reading this chapter, what additional insights have you learned about yourself and what can you do to change your life for the better?

SECTION III

WHAT STOPS THE EMOTIONAL MATE FROM CHANGING?

Do you remember Mary in the first chapter? Remember that she felt miserable in the relationship and she was tired of the struggle to change Phil? Let's catch up on the rest of her story. Mary wondered why, no matter what she did to improve the marriage, her words would fall on Phil's deaf ears. There was very little communication with Phil and he acted as if he was in another world. Life at home was dreadful and Mary could not encourage a response from Phil to make a difference. "There is no getting through to him. It is so frustrating I could scream," Mary shared her anguish. "Only after I get upset and yell or cry would Phil make some changes, but he would change for only a short time. To make it worse, every time I would become upset to get my point across, it seemed he would eventually use my feelings against me, telling me I had the problem." She continued, "Even if I tried to be a good Christian wife and give love and affection to encourage him to change, he just stayed the same. This has been going on for so long, I'm at the end of my rope and I don't know what else to do."

REASONS WHY THE EMOTIONAL MATE DOES NOT CHANGE

If you are living in an emotionless relationship like Mary, you may feel trapped in a marriage that seems hopeless to change. If you have been living in this long enough, you don't know what else to feel, but you know you don't want to feel this loneliness or misery any longer. You may have reached the point that most emotional mates will eventually arrive— caught between the decision to desperately want a change, but afraid and unaware how to take those initial steps. Let's begin by explaining reasons why the emotional mate may not make changes:

Feeling helpless to change

A primary reason you feel helpless to change your situation is the belief that you are trapped in the situation with no way out and no alternatives. This belief is a lie coming out of your past or current situation where you may have been helpless to do anything. Growing up, Mary lived in a home where something bad always seemed to happen after her parents had an argument. One of her parents would leave or get hurt. During these situations, Mary felt afraid and helpless to do anything about what happened. As an adult, Mary hates to argue with Phil because she is always afraid something bad will happen. She never realized her fears stemmed from the helplessness she experienced as a child.

Another common reason for helplessness is the feeling of being subordinate or "less than" others, especially with your mate. This can happen when your mate has a strong personality and is controlling or demanding. This feeling hinders you from believing you have a right to stand up for yourself and make changes. If you "feel" helpless, I strongly recommend you seek counseling for your situation.

Children

You may be staying in your miserable situation for the sake of your children. It is very noble that you are trying to make decisions based on the needs of others. However, you may need to take a second look at how the situation is influencing your children. Children are very perceptive and easily influenced by the environment around them. Whatever is observed and heard in the home will be the primary experiences that will teach them *what* to feel, *how* to feel, and how to *behave* the rest of their life. No matter how much you believe you are shielding your children, the emotional and physical hurts you are experiencing are also being experienced to some degree by your children. These hurts will be felt the rest of their lives and negatively affect their own future relationships. Being a loving parent does not mean you must stay in an abusive situation for fear you would be hurting the children if you change. For you to change does not always mean you must separate or divorce. However, you must be willing to stand up for what is right and stop an unhealthy situation. You may need to have alternate plans to care for the emotional and physical well-being of you and your loved ones. This may include counseling, financial assistance, and a place to stay on a temporary basis. This will be discussed more in the next chapter.

Misinterpretation of submission

The church has primarily used the Bible verses in Ephesians 5: 22–29 as the basis for the relationship between the husband and wife in a marriage. You may be familiar with the verses used most often in Ephesians 5:22–23, which state, "Wives, submit to your husbands as to the Lord. For the husband is the head of the wife as Christ is the head of the church, his body, of which he is the Savior." What you hear less about are the verses for the husband in Ephesians 5:25–27, which state, "Husbands, love your wives, just as Christ loved the church and gave himself up for her to make her holy, cleansing her by the washing with water through the word, and to present her to himself as a radiant church without stain or wrinkle or any blemish, but holy and blameless."

These verses in Ephesians are instructions of submission for both husband and wife, not just one partner. Ephesians emphasizes in Chapter 5:21, "Submit to one another out of reverence for Christ." When the instructions for both husband and wife are fulfilled, the marriage will be blessed. It will not work when only the wife tries to submit to the man and the husband does not submit to Christ. Husbands have a higher calling to love their wife as Christ gave Himself up (died) for the church. That means men must sacrifice themselves to make the marriage union as holy and blameless as possible. If he is not doing this, the husband is not fulfilling his commitment.

Colossians 3:18 and 19 clearly state the rules for the household are, "Wives, submit to your husbands, as it is fitting in the Lord and husbands, love your wives and do not be harsh with them." Submission will work for the wife only when the husband honors the wife as he commits his life fully to the Lord. The Bible interpreter, William Barclay, explains it this way, "The fundamental effect of this Christian teaching is that marriage becomes a partnership. It becomes something which is entered into not merely for the convenience of the husband, but in order that both husband and wife may find new joy and a new completeness in each other. Any marriage in which everything is done for the convenience of one of the partners and where the other exists simply to gratify the needs and desires of the first, is not a Christian marriage."[36]

Misinterpretation of scripture

Mary was told she would not be a good Christian wife if she became angry or stood up against the inappropriate things her spouse said or did. Mary wanted to be a good example for her family so she didn't want to make any waves whenever there was conflict. For anyone that feels, thinks, or acts like Mary, it would be important to understand what Jesus expects of you rather than standing on someone else's interpretation of how you should be as a Christian. The Bible is clear that Jesus wanted to change how the world prayed, thought, and behaved in their devotion toward God and relating to people. Jesus knew He was up against stubborn people who were stuck in their strict spiritual rituals that did not give glory to God. To get the message across, Jesus was emotional, bold, and compassionate.

Jesus demonstrated many emotions that you read about in a previous chapter, but more specifically Jesus teaches that you can have anger as a natural way to tell someone how you feel. However, do not let the anger get out of control where it will verbally or physically hurt others. "In your anger do not sin. Do not let the sun go down while you are still angry, and do not give the devil a foothold," (Ephesians 4:26–27). The life of Jesus is a great example of how you can show compassion for people, "Therefore, as God's chosen people, holy and dearly loved, clothe yourselves with compassion, kindness, humility, gentleness and patience," (Colossians 3:12). Show strength through your boldness when you need to get a point across. "Now, Lord, consider their threats and enable your servants to speak your word with great boldness," (Acts 4:29). There were many occasions when Jesus spoke with extreme boldness in order to put a stop to inappropriate behavior. "You brood of vipers, how can you who are evil say anything good? For out of the overflow of the heart the mouth speaks. The good man brings good things out of the good stored up in him, and the evil man brings evil things out of the evil stored up in him," (Matthew 12:34–35).

Afraid to lose the relationship

If you are afraid to fail or afraid to make the relationship worse, step back and take a good look at the situation you're living in. Ask yourself this important question: *If I stood up to my mate and he or she left the relationship because of my actions, what is it about the relationship I am afraid to lose?* If you are living in an emotionally dead relationship, you probably have little or nothing to lose. Your *relationship* is already dead! The longer you allow this relationship to remain the same, the more certain you will emotionally die, too!

MAKE CHANGES OR LIVE THE SAME OLD LIFE

Does it make sense for you to constantly ask or plead for your soulmate to show you love? Think about what you are doing! Why do you need to beg for love from someone that vowed to love you the rest of their life? Why are you letting yourself live this way? Why are you allowing your mate to emotionally neglect you and disrespect you? When you have asked, begged, pleaded, written notes, and tried everything you can think of to change your mate, with minimal or no results, you are fighting a losing battle. The truth is your own unhealthy emotions are getting in the way of thinking confidently and speaking boldly against what is happening.

Mary had to get to the point of yelling or crying from total frustration before Phil would make any small changes. She felt she was losing more than she was gaining, as if she was always on the defensive and struggling to get ahead. I told Mary that her repeated efforts would not work to change the unemotional condition of Phil. To really make a change in her husband, Mary needed to change strategies. I asked Mary if she was ready to deal with the problem. "Of course I am. I finally realized there is nothing I can do. I want to either make it better or just get out," she said with certainty.

I asked Mary, "For all the years you tried to change the situation by complaining, how much did it solve the problem?"

Her silence and the blank look on her face told the story. "Very little," she said sadly, as if I opened a door of personal hurt that would be too much to bear.

I said, "If you are ready to deal with these problems head on, you must stop trying to change your mate. Instead, work on changing how *you* are dealing with the situation." She looked at me as if I was a traitor, jumping to the enemy's side. Before I was shot for treason, I quickly said, "It is true that you have been treated poorly for a long time and you want to blame Phil for not changing. However, at this point, you will not make a difference by telling Phil to change or by being submissive to him."

You could see the surprised look on her face as if what I said went against the grain of everything Mary believed and understood. She admitted to being hesitant to think that way, but realized she had to do something drastically different to change the situation.

Letting go of all you have believed and felt for so many years, in order to begin emotionally separating from your mate will be one of the most difficult changes in your life. If you let go, you may be afraid the relationship will fail or your mate may leave. That possibility is always there. However, you need to recognize that *the longer you remain the same the longer you allow yourself to be disrespected and the longer you enable your mate to remain the same.* You need to make an important choice and either live with the dysfunctional relationship the way it is or change how you live and respond to the relationship. Since your unemotional mate is typically more dependent on you to maintain the relationship, you have more influence than you realize to change your situation. It's your choice to begin making changes in yourself.

WORDS OF ENCOURAGEMENT

Like with Mary, how many times over the months or years, have you tried and tried to change your situation, believing something should happen, but little occurs with lasting results? How much frustration, disappointment, and misery will need to build up inside before you seek help beyond your own ability? How helpless will you become before you will allow yourself to completely change how you approach your situation? Take heart; you are not alone. Keep reading to find the answers that will help change your life and the life of your mate.

Personal Reflection

Lord, bring to my heart how you want me to feel differently
and bring to my mind how you want me to think differently
to strive for the relationship you want me to have.

STUDY QUESTIONS

1. Describe any reasons that are stopping you from making a change.

2. What does Ephesians 5:21, "Submit to one another out of reverence for Christ," mean for you and your spouse?

3. Describe what needs to happen before you are ready to make a change?

4. Describe how your situation is similar or different from Mary and Phil.

5. What have been the biggest difficulties with trying to change your mate?

6. Are you ready to stop blaming your mate and focus on changing yourself? Explain.

7. After reading this chapter, what additional insights have you learned about yourself and what can you do to change your life and your situation for the better?

23

CHANGE THE EMOTIONAL MATE TO REVIVE THE RELATIONSHIP

~

If the emotional mate remains the same,
the unemotional mate will see no need to change.

For the emotional mate, the difficulties from living in an emotionless relationship can have a crippling affect on your ability to cope emotionally, physically, and spiritually. If you continue to live in an emotionally empty relationship long enough, most likely you will slowly succumb to the darkness of an emotional death in your heart. You may have never expected the relationship to turn out this way and you may try to cope the best way you can. Unfortunately, you end up living somewhere between numb, hurt, angry, resentful, trapped, tired of trying, or giving up. Wherever you are, these are normal feelings as a result of the type of relationship you never dreamed of experiencing. Before you live one more day this way, you need to ask yourself if you are ready to try something that is different and more powerful than anything you have ever tried.

If the answer is "yes," then the following steps can be used to help you begin changing your circumstance and receive the love and emotion that are missing in your relationship. This chapter will focus on ways to change by stretching your faith, thoughts, and behaviors. If you "feel" like you are helpless to make any changes, you need to know the truth about how much influence you really have in making a difference. If you are ready to change your relationship, you need to stop trying to change your mate and be ready to make the biggest changes within your own life. If you are reading this as the unemotional partner, you need to allow your emotional mate to make these suggested healthy changes to improve the relationship.

SECTION I
REVIVING THE HEART, MIND, AND SOUL

You will not change until the pain of remaining the same is greater than the pain of change.

If you have lived in an emotionless home long enough, you cannot help being dragged down and feeling defeated no matter how much you try to change your unemotional mate. Over time, you become confused and numb to your own emotions, becoming insensitive to your situation and eventually emotionally dead inside. One of the devastating outcomes of living with an unemotional person is the traumatic effect it has on your mind, body, and soul. In your efforts to make the relationship work, your own emotions are drained as you become a victim to the very thing you want to change in your unemotional mate. As the emotional mate, it is difficult to detect the slow emotional death inside your own heart. I cannot emphasize enough that the only way you will survive is to emotionally and physically distance yourself from the sources that drain you. In addition, you must strive to broaden your horizons outside your circumstances for answers and strength. To make any effective change, you must discover and utilize the sources of encouragement that are available to you. This is vital to providing encouragement for building up areas of spiritual, physical, and emotional strength. I will attempt to explain further what I mean by this.

RECOGNIZE WHO IS UNEMOTIONAL

If you live long enough in an unemotional relationship you struggle with identifying your own emotions, struggle with your ability to emotionally relate to others, and eventually lose the ability to recognize what feelings are normal during hurtful situations. This is why it is very important for you to recognize and learn what unemotional characteristics are before you become unemotional yourself. When Elaine came in for counseling she didn't realize how emotionally drained and mentally numb she was. Throughout the marriage, Jake didn't express feelings and would often give sarcastic comments that discouraged Elaine from expressing hers. As a result, Elaine felt she couldn't be free to be herself and was always cautious with what she said or did. Elaine never realized her being emotionally drained was the result of living in an emotionally oppressive home.

For all the years of sarcasm, Elaine became numb to Jake's disrespectful treatment and lost her own ability to feel normal emotions. I told Elaine that one priority of survival is to keep in mind who was initially unemotional. I had to remind Elaine that it was her husband who originally came into the relationship without emotions. If you think back to the beginning of the relationship, you were the one (and hopefully still are) the partner with the dream and passion to relate and connect emotionally. Like Elaine, always keep in mind that your unemotional mate is the one emotionally disabled and you are the one who has (or had) the normal emotions and the willingness to make a change. Even if your unemotional mate had passion at one time, the reason why you are reading this book is because you've tried everything to no avail and you cannot get the relationship to emotionally move forward.

One way to help yourself regain your emotions is to use the four questions found in the chapter, "How to Communicate Your Feelings":

What's going on inside?
What am I feeling inside?
Why do I feel this way?
What am I going to do with these feelings?

As you ask yourself these questions, give yourself permission to feel, and you will slowly find your feelings again. If you are in a relationship where you are not allowed to use feelings, answer these questions in private. You must give yourself permission to find your feelings to begin the process of healing yourself toward the eventual change in your circumstances.

SOURCES THAT DRAIN YOUR HEART, MIND, AND SOUL

As the emotional mate, you may not feel alive in your relationship. This is the unfortunate fallout from your situation. You must recognize the sources that drain your heart, mind, and soul. If you do not, you will continue to suffer emotionally, spiritually, and physically, and never be able to fully climb out of the emotionless world. You may find yourself drained when the following situations happen:

- You receive little or no emotional comfort, support, or encouragement.
- You receive belittling, negative, or joking comments when you express emotions.
- Your emotions are used against you in some later discussion or argument.

- You or the children receive negative or disrespectful comments.

- Your mate is irresponsible and/or does not follow through with promises.

- You have to frequently remind your mate about appointments, chores, general responsibilities.

- When you must frequently ask for help with the children and daily household chores.

- Your mate regularly forgets birthdays, anniversary dates, and special events.

- Your mate does not pick up after himself or herself—clothes, dishes, tools, etc.

- Your mate is irresponsible or too controlling with money.

- Your mate has a controlling or demanding attitude and is emotionally or physically hurtful.

- You are feeling helpless to change the situation.

- When you do not receive (or you must ask for) emotional support, i.e., hugs, kisses, etc.

DISTANCE YOURSELF FROM WHAT DRAINS YOU

Once you recognize the sources that drain you, the following are some suggestions to emotionally and physically distance yourself from those draining sources. It may be beneficial to reread the chapters, "Stop Trying to Change Your Unemotional Mate" and "How the Emotional Mate can Make Healthy Changes."

- If there is a lack of emotion or little/no emotional support from your mate, recognize your mate has a problem with expressing emotions, give *yourself* permission to express emotions, and seek emotional support from others.

- If there are belittling, negative comments, or your emotions are used against you, recognize that your mate has a problem. Give yourself permission to express your emotions (regardless of what your mate says), and seek professional help to learn how to handle the disrespectful treatment.

- If your mate insults you, recognize you do not deserve those comments. Recognize that you did the best you could and the insult was out of your mate's insecurity, not your ability. If you can, make a brief comment about how you did not appreciate his or her comment.

- Stop personalizing, blaming yourself, or trying to take responsibility for everything your mate verbally or physically throws at you. You do not deserve the disrespect your mate gives you and you are worth more than any words of disrespect.

- Do not allow anyone to control or abuse you: emotionally, physically, or mentally. (See the chapter, Stop Trying to Change Your Unemotional Mate for details).

- If you are emotionally suffering because your mate will not change, stop wasting your valuable energy trying to change someone that is already emotionally dead and refuses to change. Focus your energy on yourself.

- You must strengthen your own heart before you can have enough power to emotionally change your unemotional mate. Focus your energy on building your own emotional, spiritual, and physical strength. More details will be provided later.

WHEN YOU ARE NOT LOVED

Not feeling loved by your mate is one of the strongest and most common sources that can drain you emotionally. Men and women have different dreams, expectations, and agendas in the relationship that are often not discussed before tying the marriage knot. Even when your mate says, "I do," it does not guarantee either mate knows how to give or receive love. If your dreams and expectations for the relationship have not been fulfilled by now, chances are your mate does not understand what they are. The longer you wait for your mate to fulfill your dream, the more hurt and resentment will accumulate, destroying the chance of reconciliation in the future. When you don't receive the love and acceptance that you originally dreamed about, the disappointment can be extremely painful.

Elaine married hoping to get the love and attention she never received in her childhood. After fifteen years of marriage, Elaine stated she continued to feel empty inside, waiting to receive the love and attention from Jake. "I realized Jake acts more like my unemotional father than I want to believe," Elaine told me as she reflected about the past relationships in her life. Elaine realized she went into marriage accustomed to living in an unemotional relationship. Elaine has realized how she must be the one to start making changes if there is to be any difference in the relationship.

If you are like Elaine, you cannot expect your partner to fill an emotional emptiness that may have been the result of poor relationships in the past. Your mate can't fill the deep emotional emptiness that came with you into marriage and it is not your mate's responsibility to keep you emotionally filled. Although your mate should show you love and respect, there is a good chance your mate didn't learn how to show it. Similarly with Elaine, you may enter the relationship with a higher expectation for love and respect than the unemotional spouse knows how to give. It is only after living without that love for some time did Elaine begin to recognize the hurtful reality that Jake is emotionally unavailable. You need to fill that emptiness with a love that is unconditional and permanent. Through counseling you can discover and heal the emotional hurts of your past. Through Christian counseling, you can discover the past hurts and allow the never-failing, unconditional love of God to fill that emptiness. Once your heart is healed from the past, you can more easily recognize your emotional needs and learn how to more appropriately obtain love from your mate and others the way God originally intended. Counseling is essential for both the emotional mate and the unemotional mate to heal your individual issues.

ENCOURAGEMENT FOR THE EMOTIONAL MATE

As the emotional mate, have you been allowing your unemotional partner to drain your life? In desperation to make this relationship succeed, have you worked hard to make things right? Because of your efforts, does your unemotional mate expect you to accommodate his or her needs to the point of ignoring your own? As the emotional mate, you are expected to be a helpmate to your unemotional partner; however, there is a point where you need to draw the line regarding how much you do for your mate. Having to repeatedly strive to make the relationship work while ignoring your own needs is not considered devotion (or submission), that is called disrespecting yourself. As long as you perform most (or all) the work, the longer your mate will expect *you* to act that way and the longer you will *allow* your mate to act the way he or she does. That's right, as long as you act the way you always have, your unemotional mate has no reason to change. You are keeping your mate emotionally unhealthy! If you really care about changing this relationship, you must change yourself, change how you allow yourself to be treated, and change how you have reacted to your mate. When you change, your mate has no choice except to change with you. Here are some suggestions for making changes:

Emotional, spiritual, and social changes

Unemotional mates (especially males) tend to be more emotionally dependent on you than you are on them. However, you would never suspect this because your mate's behaviors and attitudes keep your attention focused on him or her with little time for yourself. Your mate's dependence may show up through:

1. Controlling behaviors: limiting your ability to develop personal, spiritual, and social interests. For example, making negative comments or discouraging you from spending time with friends, extended family, or church activities. (This is a form of emotional abuse.)

2. Noncommittal attitudes: showing little interest in planning, making decisions, or doing activities with you or the family.

3. Neediness or helplessness: when your mate acts like a victim or helpless. For example, your mate frequently withdraws into a silent world or complains about life being too hard, unlucky, overwhelming, or stressful. As a result, you must take on the majority of responsibilities for the family.

The longer you allow your unemotional mate to have an unhealthy dependence on you, the longer you will continue to feel unhappy and trapped. One way to change your mate is for you to get out of your own dependent behavior. Break out of your old mold and look for ways to strengthen and encourage your life. When you become stronger, you will be able to face your situation better and strengthen your relationship. If this sounds impossible, I recommend that you pray for God's strength and seek counseling to help with your own changes. Here are some suggestions for emotional, spiritual, and social strength:

- Find a local church
- Ask a pastor for friendship groups or Bible studies
- Regularly pray and ask others to pray for you
- Community Bible Studies: (Bibles studies throughout the USA Visit: www.CommunityBibleStudy.org)
- Look at the local paper for events of interest
- Pamper yourself (get a massage, get a tan)
- Join a fitness or health club
- Seek professional counseling
- Volunteer somewhere
- Write in a journal
- Call a friend
- Take a walk
- Daily prayers:

> Focus your prayers on God to change yourself. You may want to daily pray, *Dear Lord, give me a new heart and put a new spirit in me; remove my heart of stone and give me a heart of flesh.* Review the chapters, Finding Strength Through Prayer and The Emotional Mate can Make Healthy Changes.

If you feel alone and have no friend to call, you have either been living in a "controlling" relationship that has discouraged you from making friends or you have your own emotional issues (e.g., trust issues, fear, etc.) that make it difficult to get close to people. Regardless of your circumstances, I recommend you seek counseling.

Physical and economic changes

When you feel controlled and physically unable to change your situation, you will feel trapped and/or helpless. When you feel helpless, you will feel sad and depressed. These feelings are dangerous and devastating to your well-being and can be used against you by abusive and controlling mates. For you to stop feeling physically trapped, you must believe you have a choice whether to stay or leave the relationship. I am not suggesting you get a divorce. I am suggesting you learn to change the "feeling" that you are helpless and the "feeling" that you don't have any choices. You need to feel free of entrapment and *believe* you *do* have choices. This is a critical step in moving forward in a healthy way. Again I am not encouraging that you actually leave the relationship, however, having the freedom, ability, and belief that you can leave will reduce the feelings of being trapped and/or helpless about your situation. The more ways you can reduce the physical and emotional sources that may cause helplessness, the more you will move forward in a healthy way. Here are some suggestions for *feeling* stronger:

- Find sources of personal income
- Obtain your own bank account
- Spend money on yourself
- Have someone to call at anytime for encouragement
- Arrange for a place to stay if you need to get away
- Seek professional counseling

STUDY QUESTIONS

1. Describe the sources that drain your heart, mind, and soul.

2. Describe how you can separate yourself from those draining situations.

3. Describe how you have felt when you are not loved or disrespected.

4. Describe how you may change your life in the following areas: emotional, spiritual, social, mental, physical, economic.

5. What issues would you need to work on with a counselor?

6. After reading this chapter, what additional insights have you learned about yourself and what can you do to change your life for the better?

SECTION II

MAKING RADICAL CHANGES

Change on the outside will only occur as a result of brokenness on the inside.

Remember Mary and Phil from the first chapter? Mary came to the realization that her efforts to change Phil were not working. She finally realized the longer she remained the same, the longer she allowed herself to be mistreated and the longer she enabled Phil to remain the same. Mary finally recognized that there was no loving relationship with Phil and he showed little interest in changing. Mary did not want a divorce, but felt stuck in a dead end relationship that she desperately wanted to improve. Through counseling, Mary realized she had to make some radical changes in her life to begin drastic changes in the relationship.

This chapter is for the emotional mate, like Mary, who believes you have tried everything from continual prayer, begging, ignoring, anger, submission, and traditional counseling, but nothing seems to work to make changes in your situation. If that is the case, something needs to happen that is so powerful it will shock the meaning of life into the heart, mind, and soul of your emotionally dead partner. Since unemotional people are already empty inside, there is little to lose by trying something more powerful than anything you have already attempted.

THE EMOTIONAL MATE MUST
MAKE RADICAL CHANGES

Mary lived in an emotionless world for so long; she was numb to her own feelings and was resigned to living in her miserable situation because she did not know what else to do. Even if the situation became intolerable, she worked harder to try to change Phil, believing she must take on the responsibility to change the relationship. If you have tried and tried to change your unemotional mate, like Mary has tried with little or no results, then you need to wonder why you are willing to endure such misery. I have a great deal of respect for partners that are willing to endure living with an unemotional person. However, by now you should know your unemotional mate has a deep-seated problem and all your efforts have not turned him or her around. Consequently, you need to give yourself permission to let go of your mate and stop trying to change someone that does not want to change. Instead, work on changing yourself. The longer you focus on changing your mate, the longer they will blame you and the longer you will feel helpless to your situation. To make changes in your unemotional mate, you must first change yourself.

This may be a totally different way of thinking, especially if you have only focused on your mate as the reason for the poor relationship. There is no doubt your unemotional mate is the greatest influence for the emotionless relationship, but you are the greatest influence toward changing your situation. Not by trying to change how your mate thinks, feels and acts toward you, but instead changing how *you* think, feel and act toward your mate.

Before you begin making radical changes there is a word of caution. You must seriously utilize what you just read in Section I to find sources of ongoing encouragement and prayer. You must be working toward strengthening your emotional, spiritual, social, physical, and economical areas of your life. The next steps will not be easy, but they are the most important to reviving yourself and your relationship. You will benefit from any support you can receive in order to stand strong in your attempt to make the following changes.

LETTING GO

When Mary first came to my office she was crying as she told me, "After eighteen years of marriage, I realized I never really felt loved by Phil." To make matters worse Mary said she didn't feel needed now that her kids were teenagers. "All I wanted was to have a family and to be loved by my husband. But I feel like my family doesn't need me and my husband never loved me," Mary said through her tears. Mary always felt that if she stopped trying to make the relationship work the relationship would fall apart. Mary sadly realized there was no relationship to save. All her work to try and change Phil would not succeed since he shows little interest toward the relationship. Mary realized she had little to lose in the relationship if she started to let go of saving the relationship and focus on herself.

No matter how much time and effort you put into this relationship to make it work or the amount of hurt and discouragement you may feel, God still performs miracles in people's lives. However, God does not force His will on others that *choose* to live an unemotional life. Remember, as long the emotional mate remains the same, the unemotional mate has little reason to change. However, when the emotional mate emotionally and physically lets go and lets God take over, God will be able to make changes.

There is an old saying, "When you let go of something, if it comes back, it was yours. If it doesn't return, it never was yours." When you are finally ready to emotionally and physically let go is the time that God can do His best work on you and your situation. When you let go of the controls, God can take over. James Dobson in his book, Love Must Be Tough, explains the importance of allowing God to be your wisdom and strength as you move forward.

Dr. Dobson states, "Furthermore, in talking to hundreds of Christians who have seen their families torn apart, I have heard one comment with overwhelming consistency: 'I would never have made it without the Lord!' They have then told me how the presence of Jesus Christ was never more real and compassionate than during the worst of the storm, when the winds of tragedy howled around them. I have seen Him turn disaster into triumph, healing wounds and repairing hopelessly shattered relationships. But it is also true that God often uses pain and crisis to bring a sinful person to his senses. There is something about great stress that takes us back in the direction of responsibility. . . . There is a place for a deliberately conceived confrontation in a troubled marriage that may take it literally to the door of death."[37]

Your mate needs you to be lovingly tough to bring change to your situation. You are at an important crossroad. You must either decide to stay the way you are or choose to change. When there is absolutely no other way out of your helpless situation, you need to consider the option of setting your mate free. When you set your mate free, you are sending a message that you are not willing to stand for this type of relationship. For unemotional people, your actions of letting go will speak louder than words. Until you get to the point where you are lovingly tough, you will struggle with letting your mate go.

SETTING YOUR UNEMOTIONAL MATE FREE

Since the unemotional mate has little reason to change

as long as the emotional mate is willing to live with whatever the unemotional partner says or does (no matter how bad the behavior may be), *you must send a clear message that you are no longer accepting how the unemotional mate is behaving or treating you.* This takes you to the next level of change to set yourself free from the unhealthy situation and helplessness you feel. This change shows you are emotionally letting your mate go. To get this message across effectively, I suggest you take your time and write out what you want to say in a letter to your mate. Writing a letter will give you time to sort out your thoughts and save you from the difficulties of trying to tell your feelings face to face in the midst of a barrage of comebacks that your unemotional mate may throw at you. The letter may read something like the following:

Dear Phil,

I have been spending much time thinking (praying) about our relationship. I have realized I have done you an injustice. All these years I have nagged you about communicating your thoughts and feelings with me because I wanted a loving and honest relationship together. I have been very hurt and frustrated because we have not been able to have that loving relationship. Well, I've realized through all this that I have been imposing on you what I believed to be important for the children and for me in our relationship. I've realized you are old enough to make a decision whether you want to become involved with the children and with me in a loving and caring way. Even though that is what I want, I cannot force you to give that love to me. That must be your choice.

Because of how we have been living, I have realized I cannot live this lonely, miserable life anymore. I cannot continue to sit back and live in a relationship where I do not receive love or respect and there are no conversations with our thoughts and feelings. I have realized I must find ways to spiritually, emotionally, and physically grow in my life. I am saddened I cannot grow with you and that you have chosen not to grow with me. Most importantly, I cannot take responsibility for what you do anymore. I have decided to let you go and let you choose what you want to do for this relationship.

May God bless you, Mary

Date the letter and lay the original letter in an obvious place for your unemotional mate to find it when you are not around. Keep a copy for yourself. Your mate will probably be expecting some nagging note, only to find something more powerful. You want the letter to be sincere about your letting him or her go and state you are going to make changes in your own life. Be sure to use "I" statements that say what you feel and stay away from using "you" statements that are accusatory or blaming. Do not be too specific about any personal plans and do not give the impression you will be leaving. Regardless of what you write, expect the information to be used against you.

This letter represents a major change in your thoughts and behavior toward your unemotional mate. This change means you are ready to step to the next level of letting go and changing how you relate and how you are tired of "taking care" of your mate. If you write the letter and then continue fixing the relationship the way you used to, your words of "letting go" will mean nothing. Here are some strong recommendations regarding how you can change your involvement with your unemotional mate after you write the letter.

- Take care of yourself—eat healthy, socialize with positive thinking people, find emotional support, and seek counseling.

- Pray for your circumstance and your mate. In addition, pray about strengthening your wisdom to keep your confidence strong and your mouth closed.

- Stop any pleading, begging, nagging, or questioning.

- If you ask your mate to go with you somewhere and he or she says no, go by yourself or call a friend to go (and enjoy yourself)!

- Stop performing those chores for your mate that can easily be done on his or her own. This may include making lunches, washing clothes, making coffee, folding clothes.

- Sleep in a different bed if you feel you need to be separated.

- Say "no" to sex if you do not feel the desire.

- If you have children, continue functions as a family—eat dinners, watch movies, etc.

- If you are without children, it is your option to make dinner for both. If you tell your mate the time dinner will be served and he or she is not there when it is served, go ahead and eat alone.

- When your mate complains about your changes, listen, but do not argue in return. If he or she becomes loud or threatening, comment that you do not deserved to be treated this way and you will not listen as long as they treat you this way. Tell your mate you will walk away if the threats do not stop. If the threats do not stop, walk away.

- Be cordial, keep dialogue to a minimum, choose your words carefully, and act with confidence.

- Unless your mate is willing to appropriately share in conversation, do not talk about your personal frame of mind, plans, or feelings. (Your personal information will only be used against you later.)

- Identify and release your feelings with a friend, counselor, in prayer, or through journaling.

- Whatever changes your mate makes, acknowledge them with a positive remark.

- If your mate does not follow through on something you ask, do not make a comment about it. (At this point, silence will be more effective than any comments you can make.)

- If your mate asks what he or she can do to make the relationship better, tell your mate," to learn how to love and respect me."

- Do not nag your mate to get counseling, let him or her decide on their own. (You will learn more about this later.)

- If you are asked about your future plans, do not give any details. Say something like, "I am working through things in my own mind and heart."

THE UNEMOTIONAL MATE WILL EITHER GET BETTER OR GET BITTER

This new level of change will either make your unemotional mate angry or break him down. If your mate is typically a controlling, angry, or demanding person, be prepared for a counter-attack with accusations, blaming statements, or angry outbursts in order to control you. Remember, the unemotional mate will interpret your standing up for yourself as negative. You must be strong, calm, and persistent in your actions to show you are serious about wanting to change. This is especially true if the emotional mate has made statements or actions in the past about changing but did not follow through.

When the unemotional mate throws accusations at you or puts you down, do not argue back or respond defensively. Your arguing will only give your unemotional mate a foothold into verbally beating you down more. Your job is to focus on yourself and carry through with what you believe is right to make the changes for yourself. Your change will ultimately affect your mate and the relationship. As you remain consistent and persistent about your changes, your mate will interpret that you are serious about your intentions. As you become stronger and more independent emotionally and physically, your un-emotional mate's fear of losing something important will break their will. Do not give in and go back to the way you were until your mate is in counseling and making observable, consistent healthy changes for a lengthy period of time.

As you have followed through with the suggestions listed above, if your mate continues to get angrier, your mate has more suppressed hurts than you probably realized. An angry spouse is typically one that is desperately trying to remain in control as "King of the Hill." Your changes are perceived as a direct attack to his kingship. If your mate continues to show tantrums after several weeks, continue to follow through with your changes and find a healthy emotional support system. You may want to pray about going to the next level to help your mate see you are serious. If you are not in counseling by now, I strongly suggest you seek professional guidance and emotional support.

THE NEXT LEVEL OF CHANGE

It had been a few months since Mary wrote Phil the first letter. Over that time Phil showed his irritation of Mary's changing through a combination of rude comments, disrespectful actions, and periods of ignoring Mary. As difficult as it was, Mary was successful in refraining from becoming defensive and keeping her emotional distance. The more disrespectful Phil became, the more Mary would want to find other activities to maintain emotional stability and create some physical distance to reinforce her disapproval of his behavior. Mary would spend time in activities such as prayer, reading, hobbies, and visiting friends or relatives for a day to keep herself and her mind away from the pressure and stress of the situation. The times when Phil was treating Mary with respect and kindness, Mary would give more attention to Phil by talking, showing interest in what he was doing, making a meal, etc. However, Mary always maintained caution around Phil because she never knew when he might get upset.

As with Mary, when the pain of staying in the relationship is so great, you begin to think more about spending time away from your mate. Leaving for a temporary period of time is one of those points of last resort for a stronger change that can demonstrate how serious you are about your dissatisfaction with the relationship. This will also be a powerful jolt of reality to your mate. If you are the compliant, pleasing type that would not be expected to change, the action of leaving for a weekend can shake up the unemotional mate to recognize that something serious could happen. I do not quickly recommend separation, however, I have found separation can work as a radical step to create a higher level of change that must take place to shock the emotionally dead mate. It is important to realize that this type of temporary separation is not a form of abandonment, but instead a way to transform the unhealthiness of the unemotional mate who has already emotionally abandoned the relationship. When your unemotional relationship threatens the health and welfare of the family foundation, you must do something more radical to shake up that unhealthy situation.

THE NEXT LETTER

Mary realized she must go to the next level if she was ever going to make an impact. As bad as Phil treated Mary, she was not a quitter and wanted to do all she could to revive the relationship. However, she was smart enough not to be taken advantage of again and realized the need to continually focus on making choices for herself to ultimately impact the relationship. Phil had never really looked after Mary's emotional welfare and she had to start thinking of her own needs or she would become more emotionally and physically sick than she already felt. Since Mary realized all her pleading and waiting was actually enabling Phil to stay the same, it was time to write the next letter and leave for a period of time to make a greater impact.

Writing the second letter will again be a radical step to send a clear message where you stand. The intention of this letter is to clearly show that you are letting go of the responsibility to change your mate by indicating you are transferring the responsibility and decision of change to the unemotional mate. You should not tell the unemotional mate what to do, but rather, emphasize you will leave for a period to give your mate some time to make a decision about the relationship. In most cases this will be the step needed to jolt your mate into the reality of what he or she will lose if they do not make a change. Before you move to this level, you must be ready to leave for an unknown period of time. It is important you not mention "separation" without following through with your actions. With any unemotional mate, your message will be hollow if you don't follow through. One suggestion is to leave a note that says something like this:

> *Dear Phil,*
>
> *I have been spending much time thinking and praying about our relationship. I have now realized I have done myself an injustice by allowing myself to live in a situation that has been unhealthy. I really want to have a relationship with you where I am loved, respected, and can freely communicate thoughts and*

feelings. However, I now realize that a loving relationship has not been able to happen with you. I have also realized that you must make up your own mind if you want this relationship to grow and improve. For me, I cannot continue to live in a relationship where I cannot talk, feel, or relate normally with you. I cannot continue to be treated this way so I am going to spend some time away to give you enough time to pray and think about whether you want this relationship to change for the better. I will also be praying and thinking about what I will do with the relationship.

God bless, Mary

As before, the letter should be dated with the original letter in an obvious place for your mate to find it when you are not around. Make a copy for yourself. There is no standard amount of time to be absent from the home. Sometimes only a weekend will be enough to jolt your mate into believing you are serious about what you say. The whole purpose of the temporary absence is not a way to punish or get even with your mate, but rather a way to send a message you are emotionally, socially, and physically strong enough to make a radical change if it is necessary. Here are some suggestions how you should be involved with your mate after the letter is given:

- Continue to pray for your circumstance and your mate. Pray about receiving wisdom to keep your stance strong and your mouth closed when necessary.

- Continue to be cordial, keep dialogue to a minimum, and choose your words carefully.

- Do not talk about your personal frame of mind, plans, or feelings. They will only be used against you later.

- Identify and release your feelings with a friend, professional, or through journaling.

- Continue to act with confidence and do not act in unloving ways.
- Make phone calls to your mate *only* when necessary.
- When you do talk to your mate on the phone or in person, keep the conversation to an absolute minimum. State your business and stop the conversation.
- Do not let your emotions get the best of you when you are accused of something. If you know the accusation is not true, just say, "I will not be treated this way. If you continue to talk to me this way, I am hanging up." If there is no other business or they continue to accuse you, tell them you are hanging up. You must follow through with what you say.
- If you start to cry during an accusation, tell them you do not deserve this treatment and stop the conversation (or hang up if you are on the phone).
- After you hang up, if your mate calls back, try talking one more time using the same boundaries as above. If your mate continues to be disrespectful, hang up and do not answer the phone if he calls back.
- If you are afraid of the consequences of standing up to your mate, you need counseling to guide you through this process.
- Whatever positive changes your mate makes, acknowledge those changes with a positive remark.
- If you are insulted, you can say, "I do not appreciate that comment and I do not want to hear that type of language."
- Be careful when you show emotion, the more your mate will see the old "pushover" in you and may use it to push your emotional buttons.
- If your mate asks you to do something together, think about the motive before you go.

- If your mate wants to reconcile the marriage, I suggest you request these considerations:

  ≈ Marriage and individual counseling

  ≈ Attend church (together or separately)

  ≈ Use the four feeling questions in chapter, "How to Communicate Your Feelings"

  ≈ Both make a list of the emotional, physical, and spiritual needs to share with one another. Talk over the needs and find mutual ways to accomplish them. (The next sections will give more details.)

During this level of change, you will be walking a tight-rope in how you treat your mate. On one hand you want to show confidence and set boundaries with how you are treated, but on the other hand, you don't want to be disrespectful in your actions toward your mate. For example, if your unemotional mate makes a rude comment such as, "The only reason you are living somewhere else is because you don't care about our family." Or, "You're the problem. You're the one breaking up the family!" Those types of comments are very common and are primarily used to get you to feel guilty and push you into an argument. Instead of responding with a rude comment, it's best to say nothing. If you must respond, try to use less emotion and make a factual comment on the inappropriateness of what they are saying, rather than making sarcastic comments about your mate as a person. You can say statements such as, "Those uncaring comments are why I am doing this. I don't understand why I am being treated this way," or "I don't need to listen to more of your rude comments. I don't appreciate your comments, and I will not continue to talk with you if you talk that way with me."

Ideally, you want to build a connection to bridge the gap in your relationship. Your unemotional mate will either break down because of your abrupt changes or continue with inappropriate behavior to see if you will fall under pressure. The more anger the unemotional mate has inside, the more stubborn he or she will be to change. You need to find a strong, emotional support system that can help you through this. This is why prayer, positive minded friends, church support group, and counseling would be extremely important.

Over the next weeks and months, if you still do not find your mate willing to change, you must make a decision to leave for a longer period. Your mate will often watch to see what you do before he or she decides to change. Returning home after a brief period can give the message that you are giving in (again). This is especially true if you have a history of giving in when your mate counterattacks. Long-term separation often does not accomplish much toward reconciliation without both partners actively working on issues through counseling. However, living in separate places can make it easier to foster better relations between each other, which can also help the counseling efforts. Child visitation schedules and money compensations, such as child support may need to be arranged if there is a longer period of separation. The "giving up" of money can bring out the worst, particularly in selfish, unemotional people.

DO NOT MAKE RASH DECISIONS

My office schedule is full of couples that enter into counseling after divorce papers have been filed. I am not naive to the fact that human nature will push a hurting spouse to the point of making decisions about divorce that will be contrary to the Bible and wise counsel. I recognize that people will get to the point of separation and divorce because they are so hurt, resentful, and fed up they will not allow a counselor or the power of God to be a part of the solution.

When the emotional mate feels so trapped and miserable

they begin to give up, often times divorce is believed to be the only option to solve the problem. My experience has shown that divorce is not typically a better solution and often a worse solution for children. I do not typically recommend divorce with emotionless relationships since the Lord can use the most painful times in our lives to work out issues that we would not normally deal with otherwise. This is where a very direct and experienced Christian therapist, utilizing the power of God, can help straighten out what life has messed up. Although God can move in the most hardened of hearts, change will only happen when the heart is open enough to allow God to work through the circumstance. You must be open to what God can do through those circumstances to break a hardened heart.

WHAT ABOUT DIVORCE?

Since I am aware people will seek legal advice no matter what this book recommends, I thought it would be wise to give some guidelines to prevent you from rushing into anything. If you must visit an attorney, I recommend you not make any decisions at your first visit in order that you may pray and take time to seek additional wise counsel from others. Emotions are already at an intense level, which often interferes with the ability to think rationally and make good decisions. If you feel strong enough, you can inform your mate you have seen an attorney to seek information about a divorce. Do not give too many details regarding your appointment because any information may be used against you later. After you share this information, monitor your mate's reaction over time. This can be a point when your mate will either emotionally break down or become angry.

If you have already visited an attorney to begin divorce proceedings, ask if you can hold the papers until you are absolutely sure about your decision. In other words, if you file the papers, I recommend that you do not have the papers served (delivered) to your mate at this point. You may want to use the fact that you filed as a way to shock your partner into recognizing the seriousness of the situation. Whatever you have done with an attorney, if you can, I recommend you wait a period of weeks to months to see the response of your mate and allow him or her to make changes. There are a percentage of unemotional mates that will break down at this point from the serious potential of losing something (the fear may be from fear of losing you, money, or the children).

If your mate does emotionally break down at this point, you should have the same expectations mentioned earlier (counseling, church attendance, etc.) before a decision is made to trust the changes. The emotional mate needs to continue his or her hard line approach until you see consistent changes. Do not nag about attending counseling, church, or any other requirements. If the unemotional mate refuses to go to counseling (after you ask once), then change has not taken place.

There will still be those unemotional mates that continue the relentless, hardened stance against any change you make. Your unemotional mate may become intensely angry, threaten to give up on the relationship, or actually leave because of other interests or relationships outside the marriage that may have already been established. Whatever your mate does, he or she will blame you for what happens and battle you every step of the way. You must remember you are working against all odds, doing the best you know how to improve a difficult situation. There will be three basic types of reactions that come from your unemotional partner.

One response will be that of anger. The unemotional partner will become indignant and interpret your actions as a personal attack. As a result, your mate will take a stronger defensive battle stance against you. The anger may come out in derogatory and disrespectful comments or behaviors. If the unemotional partner has always had an angry personality, he or she will continue to behave in the same way. Remember, when your partner becomes inappropriately angry, he or she is actually having a temper tantrum. You need to be emotionally strong and feel physically independent (not give in) when you comment that you do not deserve to be treated with disrespect. You need to counter the angry outbursts with calm, direct and firm comments (the less comments the better) just like you would any child having a temper tantrum. Follow the steps previously mentioned in this book if you become physically threatened or afraid of your mate.

The second response will be that of shutting down or isolation. Sometimes this response is the initial reaction before the anger comes, but often the unemotional mate will become more depressed and withdrawn (which is another way of dealing with anger). If your unemotional mate has traditionally been quiet and depressed, he or she will simply get worse. In order to get more attention, comments may be verbalized about being depressed or about life not being worth living. You should take these responses seriously and use the same process as I have described in this book to get him or her help. This will be addressed in more detail later.

The third response is when an unemotional mate emotionally breaks down because they become afraid of losing the relationship. When your mate becomes afraid of you leaving, they may break down crying, become withdrawn, ask (beg) you to stay, or become extremely nice and caring. Regardless of how your mate responds, take time to watch what happens in the relationship and do not rush into any decisions no matter how nice or irritable your mate becomes. Continue with the suggestions written previously, with these additional hints:

- Over the next weeks and months, pray and seek counseling.

- Be cautious of the advice from friends (especially people who are negative).

- Always talk, pray, or write out your feelings.

- You must stay respectful in your attitude and actions no matter how much your mate tries to counter with accusations and threatens you to see if you are serious.

- Do not let your emotions get the best of you as the barrage of verbal accusations increases.

- Continue to show distance in your physical, emotional, and sexual involvement (i.e., sleeping in another room, limited activities together, etc).

- Do not give hugs and kisses unless you really mean it.

- Do not have sexual relations if you do not want to.

HIGHEST AND MOST RADICAL CHANGE

A high percentage of emotionally dead mates break down after they are served divorce papers. The surprise of actually losing something important is often the next radical step to see if the unemotional mate will change. Either he or she will be shocked into realizing they will lose everything they have or they will dig their heels in deeper and fight until they actually lose everything. Since the unemotional mate cannot relate emotionally and doesn't possess skills to keep a relationship going, the unemotional mate is very dependent on the emotional mate to maintain the relationship. As a result, if the emotional mate were to leave, it is often the case that the unemotional mate would typically crumble (unless they get angry first). The potential for losing what they have in the relationship will hopefully break open the hardened heart and awaken any small glimmer of emotion still shining within their heart.

If there is even the smallest spark still smoldering inside, filing for divorce can be such a strong dose of reality that it has the potential to push the unemotional mate to the breaking point of change. When both partners are willing to work together, there is still the opportunity to reconcile a broken relationship in the middle of divorce proceedings. However, it is often the case that by the time you file for divorce, you may be so fed up and worn out, you usually want out of the relationship. If each partner does not find constructive ways to let out the hurt and bitterness, it will drive a wedge between any possibility of reconciliation. Whatever direction you decide, you are strongly recommended to seek counseling before, during, and after your decision.

BROKEN ENOUGH TO CHANGE

The burning question for emotional mates is why it must get to the point of losing everything before the unemotional mate will consider changing. If the unemotional person's heart is as hard as a stone, it requires something stronger than a stone to break it open. Just as you could never bend or break that stone with your bare hands no matter how hard you tried, you cannot change that person's heart, no matter what you say. Just as you could not break that stone until you crushed it with the force of a sledgehammer, circumstances must get to the point of a sledgehammer when you cannot get through any other way.

As you have learned in this book, emotionally unavailable mates relate more with the head rather than with the heart. As a result, change must come through strong prayer, logic, patience, calm but firm actions, and a radical change, in order to break the heart of stone. I believe God desires every unemotional mate to change, and I believe God still answers prayers for changes to happen. However, God cannot impose his will on someone that chooses not to change. For unemotional people, change starts from an outside influence that creates brokenness from within. The more radical the changes the emotional mate can make, the greater the unemotional mate will be influenced to change.

THE BREAKING POINT

Each level of change previously discussed represents a potential breaking point for the unemotional mate. Ideally, the first time the emotional mate mentions the word "leaving," the unemotional mate should come emotionally crashing down at your feet. Sadly, that rarely happens with an emotionally *dead* mate. Each of these levels represents a radical step for a higher potential of personal loss in the effort to reach a breaking point within the unemotional mate. Whether it is the result of pride, stubbornness, deep wounds, spiritual warfare, medical issues, or a combination of them all, the unemotional mate can be resistant to what would seem to be the best thing for them. As I previously stated, unemotional people will not change unless there is a great enough threat (or actual loss) of losing something of high enough value.

This is a difficult concept to understand for unemotional people that do not have feelings and are filled with hurt or anger. Even if making changes is the best thing to do, the hurt inside blinds the unemotional person from being able to logically grasp their need to change. However, the unemotional person has lived this way for so long, they must be shocked into realizing the importance of what they will lose, if they do not change. Ideally, when the unemotional person gets to the point of losing what they believe to be important, that *should* be the turning point.

What will be important enough to the unemotional mate to lose before they are willing to change? Will he or she need to lose their home, children, or a spouse? There is a point at which everyone becomes broken. What is the breaking point for your mate? As the emotional mate, you may not find the answers to these questions until you start making changes in your own life.

≈

STUDY QUESTIONS

1. How will the emotional mate feel and respond if the unemotional mate does not change?

2. What needs to happen before the emotional mate is ready to let go of the unemotional mate?

3. How would the emotional mate know when leaving is an option?

4. What would need to happen before the unemotional mate is broken enough to change?

5. After reading this chapter, what additional insights have you learned about yourself and what can you do to change your life and your situation for the better?

SECTION III
STANDING UP FOR YOURSELF

The more you change, the more your mate will change.

The longer the unemotional mate has been unemotional, the longer he or she will consider the emotionless life as normal. The unemotional mate expects the emotional mate to provide for their needs, overcompensate for their shortcomings, remain silent about emotions, and allow everything to remain the same. For the sake of you and your family's emotional well-being, you cannot afford to allow this to happen any longer. This section is to help you understand how the unemotional mate will react when the emotional mate begins to make radical changes.

As the emotional mate, your changing for the better may be demonstrated through becoming less afraid to stand up to your mate, less afraid of the future without your mate, less afraid that you will be the cause (blame) if anything happens to your marriage, less afraid to ask questions, and less hesitant to verbalize your feelings regardless of how your mate will react. No matter how much you begin to change, your mate will interpret your feelings as irritating, talking back, getting even, disrespectful, or you are trying to get "one up" on them. The truth is, as you feel better about yourself and stand up for yourself, your mate will interpret the changes as if *you* are getting worse or you are against them. (This will be explained in more detail later in the book.)

THE UNEMOTIONAL MATE WILL NOT LIKE CHANGE

One important piece of information you need to remember throughout your changing is: *As you get better, you unemotional mate may act worse.* The unemotional mate is so accustomed to living without emotions and expecting everything to stay the same, your change will be confusing and threatening. Let me explain. If you have acted the same way for years and you suddenly begin to stand up for yourself and act differently, your unemotional mate will not like the change. Think about it. Let's say that over the years you've been a quiet and submissive wife and your husband has habitually become upset or shut down if you didn't do what he asked. Suddenly, you start to verbally stand up for yourself by telling your husband that you don't like how you're being treated and how you don't appreciate his silence or rude comments. These changes are actually a sign you're getting better. However, since you are not the submissive wife anymore and your husband thinks he is losing control over you, he will interpret your changes as if you are the one with the problem.

The more controlling your mate has been in the past, the more your mate will not like you standing up for yourself. You may receive more inappropriate comments, controlling behaviors, or see an increase in isolating behaviors in order to regain the control your mate believes has been lost because of your changes. As you stand up for your needs, your mate will try to force you back into the type of person you were before. The fact that your mate is fighting back is a confirmation you are making a difference in your mate's life. Don't fall back into the helpless person you were before. Keep changing and becoming a healthier you.

Remember, you are not focusing on trying to change your mate by telling him what to do. You are to only focus on changing yourself by becoming spiritually and emotionally stronger and expressing your own feelings and needs. Just by the very nature of you changing, you will make a great difference in the relationship. For example, if your mate repeatedly shuts you out or walks away when you want to talk about important issues, you have a right to say what you feel about being disrespected and ignored. (Use the steps in the chapter, How to Communicate with Your Mate.)

If your mate is not accustomed to you standing up for yourself, be ready for him or her to either ignore you more or make derogatory remarks. These reactions are sure indicators you are starting to make a difference and your mate is beginning to change. At this early stage, instead of getting defensive from the behaviors or insulting remarks of your mate, it is best to respond with a direct and simple response such as, "I didn't appreciate your comment and do not want you to say that to me again." If your mate responds by walking away, do not run after them. If you do not know what to say, then say nothing and walk away. You will *not* win through arguing. Saying what you feel, saying no, and standing up for yourself are interpreted as insubordination and a direct challenge to the unemotional mate's way of life. Since your mate will not understand what is happening when you change, you will see more anger, silence, confusion, and/or defensiveness. Becoming defensive through anger or shutting down is a way for the unemotional mate to feel in control, maintain superiority, or deal with feelings of insecurity. When you change for the better, it is similar to raising your status in the relationship, challenging your mate's status as king.

PLAYING KING OF THE HILL

Have you ever played "King of the Hill" as a child? This is where one child stands at the top of the hill as the king and everyone else stands at the bottom of the hill. The goal is to run up the hill and push the king off the top so you can become the new king. The King of the Hill must be ready at all times to defend their position and fight off anyone challenging the spot as king. This is the type of game you are going through with your mate. To compensate for the deep-seated sense of insecurity, the unemotional mate will defend the position as king. Telling your mate what to do is the same as challenging the position of kingship. This is why your relationship only gets worse when you remind, correct, or stand up to your mate. The more your mate feels challenged, the more he or she will have emotional tirades or shut down emotionally. These behaviors are a way of emotionally defending the position of power.

The unemotional mate's only mission will be to keep you at the bottom of the hill and defend his or her position at all costs. For example, becoming more independent, voicing your opinion, setting boundaries, standing up against disrespectful words or actions, will all be interpreted as a threat against the authority as king. In turn, your mate will try to throw you back down the hill by challenging you with a personal attack. The attack may first be with derogatory comments or actions that will discredit or ignore what you say or do. As you continue to stand your ground, the attacks will spread to accusations toward your extended family, activities outside the home, friends, church activities, or the kids. The more the unemotional mate feels threatened, the more intense the counterattacks will be to push you down the hill. I am not suggesting that you intentionally challenge your mate. Just calmly and appropriately acting different can threaten a person who does not expect the unemotional world to change. Your mission at this point is to focus on strengthening yourself into an emotionally expressive and rational thinking person that can patiently and confidently withstand your mate. Changing yourself first is the only way to make a difference. When you change, your mate will change.

NEITHER MATE SHOULD EXPECT TO BE KING

It is very important you understand that neither mate should strive to become king over the other. Ephesians Chapter 4 and 5 provide some of the best Biblical truths for a marriage relationship. Ephesians 5:21 states, "Submit to one another out of reverence for Christ." One of the best ways to have a healthy marriage is when each partner always considers the other in everything that is done. The marriage relationship is a team effort not a dictatorship. In addition, when each partner gives love and respect as interpreted in the Bible, there is a greater potential for more harmony and satisfaction. Ephesians 5:31 states the biblical marriage is to be complimentary and to build one another up to where "the two will become one flesh." Ephesians 4:29 states both partners should build one another up, "Do not let any unwholesome talk come out of your mouths, but only what is helpful for building others up according to their needs, that it may benefit those who listen."

DEFENDING THE HILL

The more the emotional mate changes, the more your mate will feel threatened and become relentless in trying to find new ways to push you back down the hill. This is why the emotional mate needs a strong emotional, physical, and spiritual support system. You also need the belief that you are good enough, the knowledge that you do not deserve this type of treatment, and the confidence and encouragement that you can succeed. The unemotional mate can become so threatened he or she will say anything or do anything to defend the position on the hill. In desperation to defend the hill, the unemotional mate may make the following derogatory, insulting, or disrespectful comments and threats about what he or she will do.

- *You've changed for the worst*
- *There's someone else in your life*
- *I don't love you anymore*
- *You're really messed up*
- *You're a terrible mother (father)*
- *Can't you do anything right?*
- *No one would want someone like you*
- *I'm going to leave*
- *You don't love me anymore*
- *I'm going to divorce you*
- *Let's get a divorce*

As you become more independent, don't give in to irrational demands and voice your opinion as you approach the top of the hill. Afraid of losing ground, the unemotional mate will intensify the counter-attack by saying or doing things to keep you at the bottom of the hill. The closer you move to the top, the more you may hear the following extreme statements.

- *I might as well not live.*
- *I'm going to take the children.*
- *I'm going to _____, and you can't stop me.*
- *I'm going to take you for everything you have.*
- *Just wait and see what happens.*
- *I'm going to kill myself.*

When statements are made about self-harm or harming others, that is an indication of clinical depression and/or they are feeling very intimidated by you (what you are doing is really working). In these situations, unemotional mates often make extreme statements for attention and maximum affect to make *you* feel worse. Regardless of the reason for the statements, I recommend you take them seriously (and call their bluff if that is what it is) by taking steps appropriate to the threat. For example, if your mate threatens their own life or others, begin to take immediate action by taking your mate to the doctor or hospital, call an ambulance, or call the police. Whatever action you take (or try to take), your mate will become irate and ask why you are doing such a thing. Because the threats are often times an irrational reaction to get attention, your mate will not understand the seriousness of what they are doing.

When your mate becomes irate from your response to their statements, do not argue. Calmly say you take those threatening statements seriously and will not play games. If you take some action after a threat, chances are your mate will not play that game again. If your mate has a history of attempting suicide or making threats, I would recommend you take it seriously and go to a doctor or have the police take them to the hospital if your mate refuses to go with you. Do not let your mate hold you hostage with emotional blackmail in order to become king over you. Emotional blackmail is a form of emotional abuse. Whatever happens, do not try to handle this all by yourself. Call your pastor, family, and/or close friend and tell them what happened.

If your mate becomes desperate to regain control of the hill, he or she will resort to more desperate measures. The motive of your mate is to keep you off the hill and stop you from getting better. In desperation, your mate may take actions such as:

- Locking you out of the house
- Emptying the bank account
- Leaving for a period of time
- Becoming increasingly nasty
- Hiding important items, i.e., car keys, letters, etc.
- Giving you the silent treatment
- Calling your family or friends and discrediting you
- Disabling the car (i.e., disconnecting the battery, etc.)
- Going to the bar (and blame you for making them go)
- Excessively or carelessly spending money

THE WOUNDED LITTLE CHILD

If you listen to the words and watch the actions of an upset unemotional mate, you will see a wounded little child. Often rebellion and defensiveness are actually an emotional temper tantrum resulting from desperation or not getting needs met. These tantrums stem from unresolved emotional childhood wounds that are triggered by current situations. This is a very common occurrence in unemotional people who do not get what they want. It can be very stressful and scary for family members to live through the emotional tirades and the barrage

of insults or threats. Adult temper tantrums may come in the
following ways:

- Pouting
- Slamming doors
- Verbal threats
- Yelling and screaming
- Stomping around
- Throwing things
- Physical abuse
- Silent treatment
- Slamming down the phone receiver
- Kicking or punching people or things
- Walking off before the conversation is over
- Withholding things and money from you

When the unemotional mate has a tantrum it is very important not to counter with a verbal or emotional outburst of
your own. The more you emotionally react the more you will
only be reinforcing the tantrums. Tantrums can be in the form
of pouting or the silent treatment. With these behaviors, I recommend that you first try to use the questions found in the
chapter, "How to Communicate with Your Mate." If giving
compassion has not worked for years, I recommend you make a
comment such as, "When you are ready to work this out, let me
know." Do not try to rescue your mate. Instead, rescue yourself
by focusing on becoming emotionally and physically healthier
and independent.

Another form of tantrum is when your mate's behavior is
disrespectful. With this behavior you need to calmly say something like, "I did not appreciate what you did and I will not
tolerate it." Since you will probably be taunted more in order
to get a reaction out of you, hold your ground by saying the
statement again, walk away, and do not respond with any other
comment. If your mate is trying to get a response from you,

saying nothing will be more powerful than any response. If you cannot hold back your own anger or bitter reaction, I strongly recommend you obtain counseling for your own issues. Do not let someone else's anger control you.

HANDLING ADULT TEMPER TANTRUMS

Coming face-to-face with an adult temper tantrum can be very stressful, frustrating, degrading, and scary. To help you, here is a way to change how you view tantrums. If you ever had little children in your house, you may have seen how they react with emotional temper tantrums when they do not get their way. As an adult, how did you handle the tantrums of those children? Did you become frightened, run away, and fall apart emotionally? If you had to correct the children, most likely you would be direct and stern with them to bring an end to the tantrum episode. You would be confident in telling them what to do and not stand for the disobedience. As an adult you would know you were correct because they were acting like a child and you needed to be the adult. The general rule with a young child is, *the more you try to explain and the more emotion you try to use, the less effective discipline will become.*

Now picture your unemotional mate having a temper tantrum. Does your mate have any of the emotional or physical reactions described in the previous list (i.e., pouting, slamming doors, verbal threats, yelling, stomping around, throwing things, etc.)? Picturing those behaviors in your mind, what childlike age does your mate look and act like? Chances are the age is under twelve years old. When your mate becomes inappropriately upset, remember you are not dealing with an adult. You are looking at an adult, but you are actually dealing with the emotions of a child. This is why you cannot rationally talk to your mate when he or she is upset. When there is a tantrum, you are actually witnessing the actions of a child. As a result, you need to explain less and use little emotion when you address your mate.

How do you react to your mate when you see a tantrum? Do you become frightened, run away, and fall apart emotionally? The only difference between the tantrum of a child and adult is that your mate is louder and bigger. Even though your mate is an adult, he or she is acting like a child and the same rules need to apply. *The more you try to explain and the more emotion you try to use, the less effective you will become.* Your attempts to have a rational adult conversation will not work when your mate is thinking and acting like an irrational child. Here are several suggestions for dealing with adult temper tantrums:

- Do not react with emotion when your mate is emotionally upset. The more emotional you become, the more you actually fuel your mate's behavior.

- Do not try to explain something when your mate is emotionally upset.

- Be direct and calm with little explanation—the explanation will not be understood during the tantrum.

- Wait until your mate has calmed down to discuss the issue.

- When you are provoked, do not provoke in return. That is childish, too. It will only be used against you later.

≈

STUDY QUESTIONS

1. What has or will happen in the relationship when the emotional mate changes?

2. Describe how the unemotional mate plays King of the Hill.

3. Describe how the unemotional mate defends the hill when you get closer to the top.

4. Describe how you observe a wounded child within you or your mate.

5. Describe how you will communicate differently when your mate has a tantrum.

6. After reading this chapter, what additional insights have you learned about yourself and what can you do to change your life and your situation for the better?

SECTION IV

WHEN THE UNEMOTIONAL MATE CHANGES

Even if your unemotional mate does begin to change, he or she will not turn into a warm loving person overnight. In fact, your mate may take weeks or months (or a few years) to change depending on the reason for the lack of emotion and the amount of motivation your mate has to change. Regardless of how expressive your mate is, you must resign yourself to the fact that your mate is emotionally disabled. If your mate is willing to make changes, he or she will need help from many other people. Most often change will come in small increments over a period of time through improved behavior and doing chores or projects around the house. As angry as you may be at your mate for not caring for your emotional needs, you still need to show respect and appreciation for the changes they are attempting to make. Do not nag or show your anger that he or she is finally learning to change after all these years. Becoming angry or getting even toward your mate will not help the situation and should not be a consideration. Being angry or nagging will only show your immaturity and make your mate angrier. Get your anger out through your own therapy, not at your mate. Here is some information and guidelines that you should put into practice as your mate changes:

- Always pray for God's guidance about everything you do

- Always write out or talk out your feelings (not to your mate at this point) whenever something is disappointing or hurtful.

- Unemotional males may initially show changes through chores or tasks. The task-oriented male will think he is changing through what he accomplishes rather than responding through his feelings. Do not expect feelings to change right away.

- Unemotional females will tend to show changes in her attitude and how she expresses herself emotionally or with doing more chores around the home.

- Your mate will expect to receive acknowledgements after doing something good or different. If you want your mate to continue changing, provide positive statements, such as: "Good job. I appreciate it when you do that. It is helpful when you do that for me. I like it when we do this together."

- Similar to dealing with little children, the immature unemotional mate needs ongoing attention for two reasons:

  1. Attention provides reassurance that the acceptable behavior is being demonstrated and encourages the behaviors to be repeated.

  2. Positive attention is what your mate needs.

- Your mate will continue to test the boundaries, the expectations, and the requests of the emotional mate. For example, out of selfish habit, your unemotional mate may watch a football game instead of spending the time he promised to spend with you. If your mate gives you a hard time after you calmly ask if you'll be spending time together, leave the room and plan to do the activity without your mate. Do not sit around stewing about what he or she just said to you. You do not deserve to have your day ruined by the immaturity and insensitivity of your mate. Get your feelings out and move on to something else that you enjoy.

- Healthy emotions will only be revealed by the unemotional mate when the unhealthy emotional or physical issues are resolved and healed. These unhealthy emotions may be from unresolved emotions of hurt, disappointment, anger, abandonment, resentment, and unforgiveness from the past or present.

THE UNEMOTIONAL MATE NEEDS HELP

Even though you have been telling your mate for years what you emotionally and physically need, you will have to say it again. The lack of emotion hinders your mate's ability to understand how to respond to your needs and desires. As with any person, if there are rewards and consequences during the learning process, you will learn faster. The same is true for your mate who should receive rewards and consequences if responsibilities are not carried out. Anyone can learn if they choose to learn and if they choose to change. Here are some suggestions for both partners to help each other:

- When something is attempted but had poor results, give encouragement for the effort. Later on you can give suggestions how to do it differently. Let the other know you liked what happened with words such as:

> "I appreciate it when you . . ."
> "It feels good when you . . ."
> "Do that more often, I like it when you . . ."
> "Thanks for (making dinner, picking up your shirt. . .)"

- The more words of encouragement you give, the more you will support the effort and encourage the attempts.

- Comment positively on the effort when you see even the smallest changes.

- Give a hug for no reason after a positive effort (be careful with giving hugs, since unemotional men may interpret that gesture as you are wanting to have sex or everything is back to normal in the relationship).

- For a reward, take your mate out for dinner or make a favorite meal.

- Go with your partner to an event they like or sit and watch a movie with your mate without being critical.

- Give compliments and don't criticize or use rude comments.

KEEP SETTING BOUNDARIES

The emotional mate needs to give acts of kindness, but simultaneously set boundaries and stand firm with what you will or will not tolerate from your mate. For example, it is often the case that as soon as you are glad for the positive changes in your mate, you may show a positive response by making a favorite meal, act nice, or give hugs and kisses. If you show kindness or encouragement before your mate's heart has started changing, your mate may interpret those positive responses as if everything is back to normal and he does not need to make anymore changes. As a result, your mate may eventually return to the former selfish and emotionless behavior. Changing yourself by remaining cautious to the behaviors of your mate is a tiring, twenty-four hour job.

WHEN IT IS HARD TO GET EMOTIONALLY CLOSE TO YOUR MATE

After years of living (or suffering) in an emotionless relationship, you may find it difficult to get emotionally close or accept love. Here are a few reasons why you may have difficulty accepting love:

Hurt, anger, and unforgiveness will hinder your love

Any unresolved hurt, anger, resentment or unforgiveness that is held in will make it difficult to get close. The anger and resentment you feel inside will make it difficult to forgive your mate and interfere with acceptance of hugs, kisses, or other forms of affection. Your unforgiveness will make it difficult for you to accept kind words or apologies from your mate. It is imperative that you work through the hurt feelings if you want to rekindle a healthy relationship. Use a journal to write out your feelings, pray to let go of the hurt, and seek counseling.

An emotionless relationship is all you know

As odd as it may sound, if you grew up in a home where emotions were not allowed, you would tend to be more comfortable in a relationship without emotions and you may not know what it is like to feel love and affection. You will always want something better, but you would not know what to do with a close emotional relationship when it happens. Because your desire for a close relationship is so strong, you believe you would gladly embrace the love that your unemotional mate would give. However, you would tend to be uncomfortable with love, similar to what you read in the charter, "Dancing the Relationship Tango." Since you are so accustomed to emotionless relationships, you will tend to feel uncomfortable with a mate that emotionally pursues you. When you receive affection from your mate, give yourself permission to enjoy that attention.

Your relationship is not physically or emotionally safe

If you have been living in a relationship that is physically threatening or abusive and you have felt scared or anxious, you may have a difficult time getting close when your mate improves. It would be very understandable for you to be hesitant to suddenly open your heart to a partner that had made you feel afraid for many years. Even if your unemotional mate is making heartfelt changes, it will still take time for you to let go of your fears. You need to seek counseling to find out why you are feeling unsafe and let go of the fear.

WORDS OF ENCOURAGEMENT

You may have been experiencing the emotionless life for so long that you may be at a critical point and want change as soon as possible. You must remember *change is a process, not like a light switch*. It may take weeks, months, even a year or more for permanent changes to happen. The amount of time it will take for changes to happen with either mate usually depends on how much accumulated anger and emotional wounds (and stubbornness) are getting in the way. Once the emotional mate starts making changes, the unemotional mate will usually start changing. Although the changes may not happen exactly how you expect, changes will take place. Always allow God to work in small steps and try not to impose what you believe should happen on what God is trying to do. Change will often be hard to recognize because it will happen in ways you would not expect. Find emotional, physical, and spiritual support each step of the way.

≋

STUDY QUESTIONS

1. What would the emotional mate look for when the unemotional mate changed?

2. Where should the emotional mate get support, strength, and guidance to remain strong through this process?

3. How must the emotional mate be cautious when rewarding the unemotional mate with kindness?

4. What may make it difficult for the emotional mate to accept changes?

5. After reading this chapter, what additional insights have you learned about yourself and what can you do to change your life and your situation for the better?

THE REST OF THE STORY

Remember the story in chapter one when Mary felt alone, empty, and miserable from the lack of emotional connection with Phil. She yearned for someone to share the burdens of her heart and the treasured moments of her day. She wondered if having those heartfelt conversations would ease the emptiness and improve the relationship. Mary believed it was possible to have close relationships, but couldn't understand why it was such a struggle to make it happen.

After reading this book, praying differently, attending counseling, and becoming confident with identifying her own feelings, Mary realized she had to make a decision to stop trying to fix Phil into the man she expected him to be. This was evident when she said, "Maybe I will not have a marriage exactly the way I wanted, but I certainly don't need to live the same way." When she decided to focus on caring for herself, become what God wanted her to be, and let go of trying to fix Phil, it freed Mary in a way she had not experienced before. Mary realized that these changes would not be easy and could take awhile to accomplish the necessary changes in herself and her relationship. However, she finally understood the importance of taking care of herself in a healthy way, finding positive emotional support, becoming more open with her thoughts and feelings, standing up for what she believed, and setting boundaries with disrespectful behaviors from others. She focused on growing in the emotional, physical, and spiritual areas of her life. She developed a stronger, personal relationship with Jesus Christ. Mary learned how valuable, loved, and accepted she was from what Christ has done and said about her, rather than basing her beliefs on what others said about her. Mary realized it was necessary to make these radical changes in herself to produce drastic changes in the relationship.

However, all these changes did not sit well with Phil. When Mary first started setting boundaries and expressing how she felt, Phil became quiet and withdrawn. After Mary told Phil her feelings in a letter, Phil blew up, making all kinds of accusations that she was not a good Christian wife and she was ruining the marriage. Over the next several months, Mary continued to find spiritual and emotional support to stand firm against Phil's barrage of negative comments.

Mary had been asking Phil for so long to change that her comments didn't seem to faze him. It wasn't until Mary was emotionally strong enough to make radical changes, such as sleeping in another bedroom, writing a letter about how she felt, and leaving home for a week, did something in Phil begin to break. Phil had to actually experience the loss of something important before he would seriously consider that he needed to change. Even when Phil began seeing a counselor and started acting nicer, Mary continued to sleep in another room and stood firm about being treated with respect and love. Mary also realized that she needed to treat Phil with respect and give him praise and encouragement. As Mary and Phil received counseling together, they learned to put aside their selfish needs, defensiveness, and unrealistic expectations and focus on how they could personally change for the good of the relationship rather than trying to change the other person.

If you want to make changes like Mary or Phil, begin looking at what you need to change within yourself before you try to change the other person. Although this may be one of the hardest things you will ever do, remember you are not alone. Philippians 4:13 says, "I can do everything through him who gives me strength." Make sure you find strong spiritual, emotional, and professional support to help you through these changes. You can make a difference!

APPENDIX

—

HOW TO FIND A COUNSELOR

It may be helpful to seek a licensed counselor with a master's degree or PhD education that has at least three years experience working with your type of situation. Since you are paying for these services, you have a right to seek the best help and ask any questions to find the right counselor.

Search for a counselor through:

- Local telephone directory under the headings: *Counselor, Marriage and Family,* or *Mental Health.*
- Web search engine (Google, Yahoo, etc.): Type in your town, your state and the words, *Family counselor,* or *Mental health counselor.*

Suggested questions to ask when seeking a counselor:

- Do you have a Master's degree or PhD in counseling?
- If you prefer Christian counseling (I recommend you do), you can ask: Are you a Christian? If yes, how do you practice Christian principles in your counseling?
- How many years have you counseled people who have difficulty expressing emotions?
- Do you have experience counseling someone who is living with an unemotional person?
- Do you work with alternative medicine, such as homeopathics?
- Do you have experience counseling people affected by diet, sleep deprivation, depression, ADD, and substance abuse?

- Do you counsel with each mate separately and with the couple together?

- If I see you alone, will my information be kept confidential from my spouse?

- Will you be honest and tell me when you cannot help my situation and refer me to someone who can?

- Does my insurance cover your services?

Suggestions for personal development during counseling:
- How to overcome anxiety and fears
- Assertiveness training
- Overcoming fear of conflict
- Conflict management
- How to say no
- Standing up for myself
- How to identify what I feel
- How to express feelings
- Resolving anger and bitterness
- Finding forgiveness
- Learning how to give and receive love
- Dealing with depression

WHAT ARE YOU
FEELING INSIDE?

ENDNOTES

~

[1] Goleman, Daniel, *Emotional Intelligence,* New York, Bantam Books, 1995, p., 52.

[2] Goleman, Daniel, Ibid., p., 53

[3] Carol Kuhn Truman, *Feelings Buried Alive Never Die...,* Las Vegas, Nevada, Olympus Distribution, p. 23

[4] Ibid. p. 23

[5] Dr. Thomas Verny, *The Secret Life of the Unborn Child,* , Dell Publishing, p. 62

[6] Ibid, p. 66

[7] Ibid, p. 49

[8] Craig Miller, *When Feelings Don't Come Easy,* Frederick, Maryland, PublishAmerica, 2001. p. 23

[9] Barbara and Allan Pease, *Why Men Don't Listen and Women Can't Read Maps,* Broadway Books, New York, NY. 2001, p. 210

[10] Bernice McCarthy, *A Tale of Four Learners,* Educator Leadership, March 1997, p. 50

[11] Ibid.p.50

[12] James Dobson, Bringing up Boys, Tyndale House, Wheaton, Illinois, 2001, p. 19–20

[13] Stephanie Shields, Speaking from the Heart. Gender and the Social Means of Emotion, Cambridge University Press, Cambridge, UK, 2002, p. 140

[14] Gary Smalley, Food and Love, Tyndale House, Wheaton, Illinois, 2001, P. 73–4

[15] William Dufty, Sugar Blues, Warner Books, New York, New York, 1975, p. 137

[16] Carolyn Dean, M.D., N.D, Complementary Natural Prescriptions for Common Ailments, Keats Publishing, 2001

[17] National Institute of Mental Health (NIMH), Publication No, 00–3561, Printer 2000, Updated: August 07. 2003, Office of Communications, Bethesda, MD

[18] Hammon, A. Christopher. "If You Don't Snooze, You Lose: Getting a Good Night's Sleep is Critical to productivity and Creativity." The QDI report on sleep and stress: a publication of The Center for Sleep and Stress on the Web. By Quanta Dynamics, inc, July-Aug. 1997.

[19] Alan, Greene, MD, FAAP, "Sleep Deprivation and ADHD," drgreene.org, Reprint, February 02, 1997

[20] Alan, Greene, MD, FAAP, Ibid.

[21] Minirth, Meier, Hemfelt, Sneed and Hawkins. *Love Hunger.* Nashville: Ballantine Books, 1990, p.26

[22] Trevor Smith, M.D., Homeopathic Medicine For Mental Health, Healing Arts Press, Rochester, Vermont, 1989, p. 16

[23] Ibid, p. 17

[24] Chappell, Peter, Emotional Healing with Homoeopathy, Rockport, Mass., Element, 1994, p., 73

[25] Trevor Smith, M.D., Homeopathic Medicine For Mental Health, Healing Arts Press, Rochester, Vermont, 1989, p. 17

[26] Chappell, Peter, Emotional Healing with Homoeopathy, Rockport, Mass., Element, 1994,p. 5

[27] Ibid. p. 5

[28] Craig Miller, When Feelings Don't Come Easy, Maryland, MD, PublishAmerica Publishers, 2001, p. 87–88

[29] Elizabeth Somer, M.A., R.D. Food & Mood, Henry and Company, New York, 1995, p. 172

[30] Harold G. Koening, MD., "Lessons Learned At Duke's Center For Spirituality Theology & Health," Christian Counseling Today, 2004 Vol. 12 No. 3, p. 39.

[31] Henry Blackaby and Claude King, Experiencing God, LifeWay Press, Nashville, TN, 1990, p 46.

[32] Laura Flynn Mccarthy, Prayer's Power Over Your Heart, Healthy Lifestyles, winter/spring 2002, p. 6

[33] Bernie S. Siegel, MD,*Peace, Love and Healing,* New York: Harper & Row, Publishers, 1989, p.29.

[34] Padus, Emrika, The Complete Guide To Your Emotions and Your Health, Emmaus, PA, Rodale Press, 1986, p., 141

[35] Ibid., p., 142

[36] William Barclay, The Daily Study Series, the Letters to the Philippians, Colossians, and Thessalonians, The Westminster Press, Louisville, KY, pp. 162–163

[37] James Dobson, Love Must Be Tough, Word Books, Waco, Texas, 1983, p. 59

Pg 144 Needs met
Pg 154
Pg 155- Spirits / Emotions
Pg 57 Sex / Emotions

You can contact Craig A. Miller at his website:
www.feelingsbook.com
or order more copies of this book at:

Tate Publishing, LLC

127 East Trade Center Terrace
Mustang, Oklahoma 73064

(888) 361 - 9473

Tate Publishing, LLC
www.tatepublishing.com